Edexcel GCSE
Religious Studies

Unit 8B
Religion and Society
Christianity
& Islam

Gordon Reid
Sarah Tyler

A PEARSON COMPANY

Published by Pearson Education Limited, a company incorporated in England and Wales, having its registered office at Edinburgh Gate, Harlow, Essex, CM20 2JE. Registered company number: 872828

www.heinemann.co.uk

Edexcel is a registered trade mark of Edexcel Limited

Text © Pearson Education Ltd 2009
First published 2009

13 12 11
10 9 8 7 6 5 4 3

British Library Cataloguing in Publication Data
A catalogue record for this book is available from the British Library.
ISBN 978 1 84690 423 3

Edited by Florence Production Ltd, Stoodleigh, Devon
Typeset and illustrated by HL Studios, Long Hanborough, Oxford
Original illustrations © Pearson Education Ltd 2009
Cover design by Pearson Education Ltd
Picture research by Zooid
Cover photo/illustration © blickwinkel/Alamy
Printed in Malaysia. CTP-KHL

Acknowledgements
ABACA/PA Photos, p. 100; AFP/Getty Images, p. 65; AFP/Getty Images/Cris Bouroncle, p. 65; AFP/Getty Images/Dylan Martinez, p. 15; AFP/Getty Images/J. David Ake, p. 21; AFP/Getty Images/Madaree Tohlala, p. 41; AFP/Getty Images/Ramzi Haidar, p. 109; AFP/Getty Images/Robyn Beck, p. 72; AFP/Getty Images/Shaun Curry, p. 54; Alamy/david martyn hughes, p. 38; Alamy/Inga Spence, p. 33; Alamy/John Norman, p. 87; Alamy/Pat Savage, p. 37; Alamy/Ronnie McMillan, p. 48; Angela Hampton Picture Library/Alamy, p. 45; AP/PA Photos/Eric Risberg, p. 9; ArkReligion.com/Alamy, p. 46; Arte & Immagini Srl/Corbis UK Ltd., p. 11, p. 106; Associated Press/PA Photos/Ariana Cubillos, p. 62; Associated Press/PA Photos/Rodrigo Lobo, p. 47; Bettmann/Corbis UK Ltd., p. 79; Bubbles Photolibrary/Alamy, p. 77; China Photos/Getty Images, p. 53; Columbia Tri Star/Album/akg-images, p. 25; Corbis UK Ltd./Bojan Brecelj, p. 7; Corbis UK Ltd./Chris Carroll, p. 75; Corbis UK Ltd./David P. Hall, p. 77; Corbis UK Ltd./Kazuyoshi Nomachi, p. 70; Corbis UK Ltd./Tomas Van Houtryve, p. 43; CreativeAct – Emotions series/Alamy, p. 98; David Hoffman Photo Library/Alamy, p. 88, p. 89; Digital Vision, p. 39; Ecoscene/Steven Kazlowski, p. 33; Empics Entertainment/PA Photos, p. 105; Epa/Corbis UK Ltd./Andy Rain, p. 59; Getty Images, p. 67; Getty Images/Brendan Smialowski, p. 96; Getty Images/Jean-Marc Giboux, p. 13; Getty Images/John Angelillo-Pool, p. 67; Getty Images/Scott Barbour, p. 81; Infertility Press, p. 44; JTB Photo Communications, Inc./Alamy, p. 81; Kidscape, p. 75; koh sze kiat/Shutterstock, p. 13; KPT Power Photos, p. 33; Landov/PA Photos, p. 71; Leonard Cheshire Disability, p. 21; Liz Lemon Swindle/Repartee Gallery, p. 92; LondonPhotos – Homer Sykes/Alamy, p. 4, p. 102; Mirrorpix/Getty Images, p. 68; Muslim Aid, p. 95; PA WIRE/PA Photos, p. 78, p. 90, p. 93; Peter Adams Photography Ltd/Alamy, p. 31; Photolink, p. 34; Pool/Reuters/Corbis UK Ltd./David Furst, p. 91; PYMCA/Rex Features/Marcus Graham, p. 4; Rex Features/Olivier Pirard, p. 74; Robert Harding World Imagery/Jim Reed, p. 33; Science Photo Library/Michelle Del Guercio, p. 51; Science Photo Library/Neil Bromhall, p. 24, p. 25; Shutterstock/Brian A Jackson, p. 36; Sipa Press/Rex Features, p. 99; Stringer/Getty Images/Matt Cardy, p. 90; Sygma/Corbis UK Ltd./Andrew Lichtenstein, p. 96; Thames21, p. 35; The Photolibrary Wales/Alamy, p. 34; TopFoto, p. 92; Tudor Photography/Pearson Education, p. 107; UK Transplant, p. 52; Vlad/Alamy pp. 2–3; WPN/Photoshot/Michel DeGroot, p. 61; Xinhua/Associated Press/PA Photos, p. 22.

Permissions acknowledgements
Scripture taken from the Holy Bible, New International Version®. Copyright © 1973, 1978, 1984 International Bible Society. Used by permission of Zondervan. All rights reserved. IPCI – Islamic Vision, Birmingham, UK.

Disclaimer
This material has been published on behalf of Edexcel and offers high-quality support for the delivery of Edexcel qualifications.

This does not mean that the material is essential to achieve any Edexcel qualification, nor does it mean that it is the only suitable material available to support any Edexcel qualification. Edexcel material will not be used verbatim in setting any Edexcel examination or assessment. Any resource lists produced by Edexcel shall include this and other appropriate resources.

Copies of official specifications for all Edexcel qualifications may be found on the Edexcel website: www.edexcel.com

Websites
There are links to relevant websites in this book. In order to ensure that the links are up to date, that the links work, and that the sites are not inadvertently linked to sites that could be considered offensive, we have made the links available on the Heinemann website at www.heinemann.co.uk/hotlinks. When you access the site, the express code is 4233P.

Contents

Welcome to this Edexcel GCSE in Religious Studies Resource

These resources have been written to support fully Edexcel's new specification for GCSE Religious Studies. Each student book covers one unit of the specification which makes up a Short Course qualification. Any two units from separate modules of the specification make up a Full Course qualification. Written by experienced examiners and packed with exam tips and activities, these books include lots of engaging features to enthuse students and provide the range of support needed to make teaching and learning a success for all ability levels.

Features in this book

In each section you will find the following:

- **an introductory spread** which introduces the topics and gives the Edexcel key terms and learning outcomes for the whole section.

- **topic spreads** containing the following features:

- **Learning outcomes** for the topic

- edexcel ⠿ key terms

  Specification key terms – are emboldened and defined for easy reference

- **Glossary**

  Here we define other complex terms to help with understanding

- **Activities** and **For Discussion** panels provide stimulating tasks for the classroom and homework
- a topic **Summary** captures the main learning points.

How to use this book

This book supports Module B Unit 8 Religion and Society, based on a study of Christianity and at least one, but not more than two other religions. Due to the choice of vast majority of centres, this book covers Islam but other religions than Islam can be studied for this exam.

This book is split into the four sections of the specification.

A dedicated suite of revision resources for complete exam success. We've broken down the six stages of revision to ensure that you are prepared every step of the way.

How to get into the perfect 'zone' for your revision.

Tips and advice on how to effectively plan your revision.

Revision activities and exam-style practice at the end of every section plus additional exam practice at the end of the book.

Last-minute advice for just before the exam.

An overview of what you will have to do in the exam, plus a chance to see what a real exam paper will look like.

What do you do after your exam? This section contains information on how to get your results and answers to frequently asked questions on what to do next.

ResultsPlus

These features are based on how students have performed in past exams. They are combined with expert advice and guidance from examiners to show you how to achieve better results.

There are five different types of ResultsPlus features throughout this book:

Build better answers: These give you an opportunity to answer some exam-style questions. They contain tips for what a basic ○ good ■ and excellent △ answer will contain.

Exam question report: These show previous exam questions with details about how well students answered them.

■ Red shows the number of students who scored low marks (less than 35 per cent of the total marks)

○ Orange shows the number of students who did okay (scoring between 35 per cent and 70 per cent of the total marks)

△ Green shows the number of students who did well (scoring over 70 per cent of the total marks).

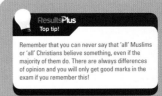

Top tip: These provide examiner advice and guidance to help improve your results.

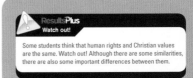

Watch out! These warn you about common mistakes and misconceptions that examiners frequently see students make. Make sure that you don't repeat them! The red, amber and green symbols highlight the severity and frequency of the error.

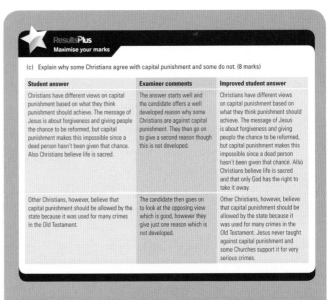

Maximise your marks: These are featured in the KnowZone (see page iv) at the end of each chapter. They include an exam-style question with a student answer, examiner comments and an improved answer so that you can see how to build a better response.

Rights and responsibilities

Introduction

In this section you will learn about the ways in which Christians work out how to make moral decisions based on the range of moral authorities available to them. These include the teachings of the Bible and the Church as well as referring to conscience and moral theories such as Situation Ethics. The section moves on to look at the ways in which rights and responsibilities are clarified within society and through the democratic political processes in the UK. The section concludes by examining the issues which arise from genetic engineering and the impact they may have on the role of individuals within society.

Learning outcomes for this section

By the end of this section you should be able to:

- give definitions of the key terms and use them in answers to GCSE questions
- describe and explain the different ways in which Christians will make moral decisions and how they will make them, including using the Bible, the authority of the Church, conscience, and Situation Ethics
- outline human rights in the UK and why they are important to Christians
- give reasons why it is important to take part in democratic and electoral processes
- explain Christian teachings on moral duties and responsibilities
- explain the nature of genetic engineering, including cloning, and differing Christian attitudes towards it
- express your own opinions on the issues covered in this section and give reasons for them.

edexcel ::: key terms

Bible	the Decalogue	the Golden Rule	pressure group
Church	democratic processes	human rights	Situation Ethics
conscience	electoral processes	political party	social change

Fascinating fact

In the field of genetic engineering, attempts are being made to use pigs' organs to grow human organs, but the human body rejects them. However, genetically modifying plant viruses can produce vaccines, hormones, antibiotics and even HIV drugs.

In pairs, or as a group, discuss what you feel to be the most important rights people have in the UK. They may be rights within society as a whole, or within your family, school or religious community. Discuss the ways in which those rights may be at risk by the law, other people or religious teachings.

At the end of the section, come back to your original list of important rights and discuss whether you would make any changes to this list.

3

The right to peaceful protest is important to many people in the UK. What do you think is the aim of this protest? How effective do you think the protest is?

1.1 Christians and the Bible

Learning outcomes

By the end of this lesson, you should be able to:

● describe what the Bible is

● explain why some Christians use only the Bible as a basis for making moral decisions

● outline the differences in Christian views on the authority of the Bible

● express your own opinions on the use of the Bible as a basis for making moral decisions.

What is the Bible?

The **Bible** is the Christian holy book. It is:

● a collection of 66 books written over hundreds of years
● divided into two parts, the Old and the New Testaments.

edexcel ⠿ key terms

Bible – The holy book of Christians.

The Old Testament was written before the time of Jesus and contains the Ten Commandments and the Law of Moses. The New Testament is concerned with the life and teachings of Jesus and the beginnings of the Christian Church.

For all Christians, the Bible is a book that carries great authority and is an important guide for decision-making. This is because all Christians believe that the Bible was inspired by God. However, some Christians use only the Bible for making moral decisions.

Activities

1 Using these teachings, explain how you think Christians would respond to the situations in the two photographs.

2 Look at the moral teachings from the Bible opposite. Do you agree with them all? List the teachings in order of importance for you. Give reasons for your choices.

3 Explain each of the points in the spider diagram opposite in your own words.

Love God	Do not murder
Do not commit adultery	Honour your parents and family members
Give to the poor and needy	Love your neighbour
Do not lie	Do not steal
Support the ways of peace	Do not be envious of others

Reasons for using the Bible as the only source of moral authority

The word of God
Christians believe that the Bible contains the actual word of God. This includes how God wants people to live their lives and worship him. By following the teachings in the Bible, Christians believe they are acting as God wants them to.

The laws of God
The Bible is filled with laws that Christians believe are God's laws on how people should act. The most famous of these are the Ten Commandments (Exodus 20:2–17).

So why is the Bible the only source of moral authority for some Christians?

The leaders of the early Church
The second half of the New Testament is about what happened after Jesus' death and how Christianity as we know it today began. The leaders of the early Church, such as St Peter and St Paul, gave moral guidance and teachings on how Christians should behave.

The teachings of Jesus
The Bible tells the story of the life and death of Jesus, whom Christians believe is the Son of God. Christians believe that they should follow Jesus' teachings and example. The Bible contains his teachings on how Christians should live their lives, such as the Sermon on the Mount (Matthew Chapters 5–7). It also contains the parables that Jesus told. The parables are basically stories that have a moral message. One of the best known is the parable of the Good Samaritan (Luke 10:25–37).

Christian viewpoints on the authority of the Bible

So why do only some Christians base their moral decisions on the Bible? The reason is that not all Christians understand the authority of the Bible in the same way.

- Some Christians believe that the Bible is literally the word of God and that God speaks to them directly through the Bible. Fundamentalist Christians believe that God directly told the authors of the Bible what to write and therefore it is totally right, without any errors.

  These Christians may argue that the Bible contains moral teachings that can be applied to all situations in the modern world.

- Some Christians believe that the Bible is literally the word of God but needs to be interpreted by the Church.
- Some Christians believe that the Bible was inspired by God and contains spiritual truths.

The Bible was written by people who were influenced by God but who were not speaking the literal truth. For these Christians, the Bible sometimes has to be adapted to be used in the modern world.

Therefore, although the Bible is an important moral authority for all Christians, there are differences about how important it is. This means that some Christians use other sources of authority when making moral decisions, either instead of, or as well as the Bible.

Activities

4 Which of the three types of Christians above are more likely to use the Bible as their only source of moral authority? Explain why.

For discussion

If Christians cannot agree on the authority of the Bible, is there any point in obeying the teachings of the Bible?

Summary

- The Bible is the holy book of Christians.
- All Christians believe it contains important moral teachings.
- Some Christians use only the Bible for guidance in making moral decisions because they believe that it is the literal word of God.

1.2 Christians and the authority of the Church

Learning outcomes

By the end of this lesson, you should be able to:

- describe what the Christian Church is
- outline how different Churches make decisions on moral issues
- explain why Christians may hold differing views on the authority of the Church
- give your own opinions on the authority of the Church.

How the Church guides Christians

We have already seen that all Christians believe that the Bible is an important authority in making moral decisions. Some Christians believe that it is the only authority. However, the Bible can be difficult to understand. Also, the Bible was written hundreds of years ago and some people believe that because of this it does not always contain answers to modern moral dilemmas. In both of these cases Christians look to the **Church** for moral guidance. The 'Church' means the community of people who believe in God and Jesus. The Church can help guide their members in making moral decisions in lots of ways such as:

- Talking to other Christians
- Listening to the priest or vicar
- Praying and worshipping God together
- Accepting the authority of the Church to explain and teach God's word

edexcel ⦂⦂⦂ key terms

Church – The community of Christians (with a small 'c' it means a Christian place of worship).

Each Christian denomination or group (such as Baptists or Roman Catholics) has authority over its members and has its own teachings, based on the Bible that members should follow. The different Churches have different ways of deciding how moral issues should be resolved.

- Some Churches discuss the moral issue in an assembly that contains people who are elected by members of the Church. After debating the issue, the assembly comes to a decision on how members should respond. The Church of England assembly is called the General Synod.
- In some other Churches, the leaders make decisions on how to respond to moral problems. Within the Roman Catholic Church, the Pope and the Council of Bishops act as the 'Magisterium', which means the teaching authority of the Church. They offer moral guidance to all Catholics throughout the world through the Catechism or from official letters from the Pope, which are known as encyclicals.

Activities

1 What kinds of things might Churches offer guidance on that cannot be found in the Bible? One might be how Christians should respond to genetic engineering. Jot down a few ideas of your own.

Activities

2 If you were a Christian, what advice would you give to the drug addict in the photograph? Why? Do you think that the Church can be of any real help to people such as these? What could the Church do in such circumstances?

3 List the kinds of problems which the Church could help with. Now make a list of those it could not. Overall, is the Church of any real use in helping with today's problems?

A drug addict.

Why does the Church have authority?

There are many reasons why the Church has authority for Christians:

- First, Christians believe that God continues to speak to them and to the world today, and that God does this through the Church. Therefore, Christians should follow the Church's teachings as they are inspired by God.
- Christians also believe that the Church is the Body of Christ. This means that through the Church, Jesus continues to act in the world today. Therefore, Christians should follow the Church's teachings as they are Christ's teachings.
- The Church is a community of believers in God. Therefore, Christians believe that God guides the Church in its moral teachings, so they should be followed.
- Although Churches have different attitudes to their leaders, all of these leaders – from archbishops and cardinals to local vicars and

For discussion

'Roman Catholic priests are all unmarried men. They should not make rules concerning human sexuality.' Do you agree?

priests – have had training and studied the teachings of the Bible and their Christian denomination for many years. This means that members of their Churches trust that what their leaders are telling them is God's will.

- Finally, many Christians would say that the Church's teachings are important because it means that Christians are sure of how to behave in certain situations. This way means that everyone knows what the 'rules' are.

Therefore, the teachings of the Church are important for many Christians. However, some Christians only use the Church's teachings as the basis for making moral decisions. Most Roman Catholics are an example of Christians who do this. They believe that the Pope and bishops have been given power by God to interpret the Bible and teach other people how to behave. Therefore, their guidance and teachings are the most important things.

Activities

4 Which do you think a Christian would say is the most important reason why the Church has authority over them? Do you agree with this? Why/why not?

5 Write a magazine article that explains to non-Christians why a Christian may only use the teachings of the Church as the basis of making moral decisions.

Summary

- The Church is the community of Christians.
- Many Christians use the teachings of the Church as a moral guide.
- Some Christians, such as Roman Catholics, only use the teachings of the Church as a moral guide.

1.3 Christians and conscience

Learning outcomes

By the end of this lesson, you should be able to:

● understand what a conscience is

● explain how a conscience can help Christians to resolve moral problems

● explain why Christians may differ on how to act on conscience

● express your own opinions, giving reasons, as well as understand how they may differ from the opinions of others.

edexcel ⠿ key terms

Conscience – An inner feeling of the rightness or wrongness of an action.

What is a conscience?

Christians believe that every human being has a **conscience**. Christians believe that conscience is given by God to us all.

> *Pray for us. We are sure that we have a clear conscience and desire to live honourably in every way.*
> Hebrews 13:18

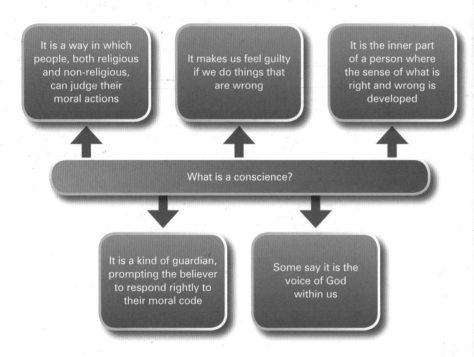

It is a way in which people, both religious and non-religious, can judge their moral actions

It makes us feel guilty if we do things that are wrong

It is the inner part of a person where the sense of what is right and wrong is developed

What is a conscience?

It is a kind of guardian, prompting the believer to respond rightly to their moral code

Some say it is the voice of God within us

Some people believe that conscience is imperfect and does not always work properly. They say that it is a useful tool to help people to decide right from wrong but that it is not always a perfect guide.

Activities

1 How would your conscience help you in the following dilemmas?

   (a) Your best friend is taking drugs and asks you not to tell anyone.

   (b) You see someone cheating in an exam.

   (c) Your friend is being unfaithful to their boyfriend/girlfriend.

   (d) You know who committed a crime but are scared to tell on them.

2 Is it right to imprison someone for being a conscientious objector?

3 **Role-play.** You are a Christian who wants to join the army but does not want to kill people. What would you say to the Recruiting Officer?

4 'Christians should fight in wars to defend their loved ones.' Do you agree?

Conscience and obedience

The role of conscience in making moral decisions is very significant for Christians. They believe that they should look at what the Bible and the Church say about a moral issue and then follow their conscience.

Therefore, Christians should never act against their conscience. For this reason many Christians have refused to fight in wars, saying that killing is against God's moral code. They are called 'conscientious objectors' because they object to fighting as a matter of conscience.

> 'A human being must always obey the certain judgement of his conscience…'
> Catechism of the Catholic Church

US Marine Stephen Funk was sentenced to three months in prison after becoming a conscientious objector and protesting about the war in Iraq.

For discussion

If conscience really is the voice of God, why don't we all feel the same way when something happens?

Was Bonhoeffer right or wrong? Why?

Acting on conscience

Christians use conscience when they are faced with a moral dilemma. For example, although abortions can be obtained legally, no doctor would be compelled to carry out an abortion if their conscience tells them that abortions are morally wrong.

If a Christian thought that they had heard the voice of God commanding them to kill a brutal dictator, they would see that the Bible says that it is wrong to murder. However, the dictator may be murdering hundreds of innocent people. To decide what to do and what teaching to follow, the Christian would use their conscience, which would probably tell them that murder is wrong and that Christians should never use wrong means, whatever the end result might be. This happened in real life, when Dietrich Bonhoeffer, a Christian, joined a plot to assassinate Hitler. The plot failed and Bonhoeffer was executed.

ResultsPlus
Exam question report

What is conscience? (2 marks) June 2007

How students answered

Few students knew nothing about the term.

Some students gave an answer which was partly correct, such as 'Conscience is something in your mind'.

The majority of students gave a fully correct definition: 'Conscience is an inner feeling of the rightness or wrongness of an action'.

Summary

- Christians believe that conscience is given by God.
- Christians use conscience as a moral guide.
- Some Christians differ as to the exact reliability of conscience.

1.4 Christians and Situation Ethics

10

edexcel ⠿ key terms

Situation Ethics – The idea that Christians should base moral decisions on what is the most loving thing to do.

Social change – The way in which society has changed and is changing (and also the possibilities for change in the future).

What is Situation Ethics?

Situation Ethics is a Christian approach to making moral decisions. It was put forward by the American Christian minister Joseph Fletcher during the 1960s, a time of great **social change**. He suggested that:

● Love should be the only principle upon which to make moral choices.
● A good action is one which aims to do the most loving thing. It is based on the simple teachings of Jesus, 'My command is this: Love each other as I have loved you' (John 15:12).
● A person should only obey the rules in the Bible or of the Church if that teaching results in the most loving thing to do.

There are several verses in the New Testament which stress the importance of love in making choices.

● 'Love the Lord your God with all your heart, and with all your soul, and with all your strength and with all your mind: and love your neighbour as yourself' (Luke 10:27).
● 'Greater love has no man than this, that a man lay down his life for his friends' (John 15:13).
● 'And this is his commandment, that we should believe in the name of his Son Jesus Christ and love one another, just as he has commanded us' (1 John 3:23).

Fletcher was clear about the kind of love that should be applied – agape love, which is an attitude towards people rather than a loving feeling. To show agape love makes it possible for someone to love their enemies and to act in loving ways towards people who have not done anything to deserve that love.

Activities

1 In a group, or in pairs, discuss how Situation Ethics may be used to solve the following dilemmas. Remember you are asking: Is there an ethical rule which should be applied or is there a more loving way?

(a) A 15-year-old girl is pregnant after being raped by a family member.

(b) A dying man asks his wife to help him to commit suicide.

(c) A woman in a prison camp would be released and allowed back to her family if she became pregnant by a prison guard.

(d) A woman could save many people from enemy attack if she were to kill her crying baby who is in danger of giving them away.

Why do some Christians use only Situation Ethics?

Many Christians would use Situation Ethics along with other ways of making moral decisions, such as using their conscience or following the teachings of the Bible and/or Church. However, some Christians only use Situation Ethics as their guide to moral issues and would therefore always act in what they think is the most loving way and will lead to the best outcome. This is because:

- Situation Ethics is very similar to the 'Golden Rule' which Jesus taught was the most important guide to the way that Christians should lead their lives: '... *do to others what you would have them do to you...*' (Matthew 7:12). Most people would want to be treated in the most loving way, which is at the heart of Situation Ethics.
- Jesus himself seemed to follow Situation Ethics when he ignored the teachings of the Bible to act in a more loving way. There is an example in the painting on this page, in which Jesus did not follow the Laws of Moses.

Does it work?

Many Christians believe that Situation Ethics has some good points because every situation is judged individually and has a genuinely Christian intention.

However, many would point out that there are some good points:

- It depends on our being able to predict what will happen, which is impossible in every case.
- In theory, anything (adultery, murder) a person felt was the 'most loving thing' could be justified.
- It is easier to apply Situation Ethics in extreme cases where there is no law to cover the situation, but it is not so easy in everyday cases where we are used to having rules.

Activities

2 Jesus carefully defused the potentially violent situation shown in the painting, protecting the woman and restoring peace. He offered a more loving way. Did he go against the law, or did he teach it? Explain your answer.

Jesus suggests that the adulterous woman's accusers search their own conscience (John 8:1–11).

3 As a group, discuss whether you understand what agape love really is and whether you have experienced anyone showing you this kind of love.

Think of well-known people, such as Mother Teresa, who might be good examples of agape love, and discuss whether you think they are good role models.

Summary

- Situation Ethics is a Christian approach to moral decisions based on acting in the most loving way.
- Some Christians only use Situation Ethics as the basis for making moral decisions.

1.5 Christians and the variety of moral authorities

Learning outcomes

By the end of this lesson, you should be able to:

- explain how most Christians use a variety of authorities to help them to resolve moral problems
- explain why Christian views may differ on the nature of authority
- express your own opinions, giving reasons, as well as understand how they may differ from the opinions of others.

edexcel key terms

Pressure group – a group formed to influence government policy on a particular issue.

ResultsPlus
Build better bnswers

Explain how Christians make moral decisions. (8 marks)

■ **Basic, 1–2 mark answers**
These answers will offer just one source of moral authority, such as 'using the Bible'.

● **Good, 3–6 mark answers**
Answers will get 3 or 4 marks that offer two sources of moral authority with reasons; 5- or 6-mark answers will either contain two sources of authority with highly developed reasons or 3 sources of authority with reasons.

▲ **Excellent, 7–8 mark answers**
The best answers usually give four sources of authority with brief reasons why Christians use them to make moral decisions. Alternatively, they might give fewer sources but explain the reasons in greater depth. Most will mention that most Christians use a combination of sources for making moral decisions.

We have looked at four different authorities that Christians use when making moral decisions:

- They follow the laws and teachings of the Bible.
- They follow the teachings and guidance of their Church.
- They use their conscience.
- They use Situation Ethics and work out what is the most loving thing to do.

Although some Christians will use just one of these authorities, most will use more than one of these sources to help them. Moral dilemmas are rarely simple, so these Christians believe that consulting all the authorities available to them is the only way of ensuring that they make the best decision.

For all Christians what is important is behaving in the way that they believe God wants. To be a Christian means living life according to God's will. The different views are there because different Christians believe that God's will is contained in different authorities or a combination of them all. For example, if Christians believe that the Bible is literally true and contains everything people need to know about how God wants them to live, they are likely to use only the Bible as the basis of living their lives and making moral decisions. Other Christians may believe that although the Bible contains the basic truth of what God wants, it should not be followed exactly as it is written and they are likely to use the guidance of the Church when making moral decisions.

Activities

A Christian praying.

A mother feeds her severely malnourished child in a shelter.

1 **Role-play.** You and your partner are Christians wondering how to serve God. You decide to spend time in prayer and worship and your partner decides to work with the needy. How would you explain your reasons to each other?

Spirit or society?

These different authorities are not used just to make moral decisions, but provide guidance on how Christians should live. Here are some different viewpoints on how Christians may believe they are doing God's will:

> As a Christian, I am concerned with my spiritual development, not with society.

> Christians must show love for their neighbours

> The Bible says that we will be judged by how much we love God, not by our work in society

> Christians have a duty to help the poor and needy of our society

> Being a Christian is about worshipping God

> Christians ought to do good works – just like Jesus did

> Christians should campaign for a fairer society

For discussion

'Christians should love their neighbour more than anything else.' Is this true?

For many Christians, performing good actions is of vital importance in living a moral life. For them, it is not sufficient just to say that they have faith in God. They put their faith into action, for example by helping the poor and needy, doing voluntary work and campaigning for fairer treatment for everybody.

Sometimes, Christians form **pressure groups**. A pressure group is one which campaigns for or against a particular issue, for example against poverty or injustice.

However, a significant number of Christians feel that Christianity and moral development should be concerned with spiritual, rather than social issues.

These Christians will concentrate on having a closer relationship with God through prayer.

Summary

- Christians believe that there are different sources of moral authority and most use a combination of these when making moral decisions.
- Christians use the Bible as the supreme moral guide.
- Some Christians differ as to the exact nature of moral authority.

Activities

2 Do you think that a Christian should spend more time on their own spiritual needs, or on looking after the needs of others? Explain your view.

3 'God wants prayers, not deeds.' Do you agree?

1.6 Human rights in the UK

14

Learning outcomes

By the end of this lesson, you should be able to:

- understand the nature of human rights
- describe government actions to protect human rights in the UK
- explain the importance of maintaining human rights
- express your own opinions, giving reasons, as well as understand how they may differ from the opinions of others.

What are human rights?

The United Nations Declaration of Human Rights says that all human beings are born free and equal in dignity and rights.

Human rights are basic rights and freedoms to which all human beings are entitled. The UK is a member of the European Convention on Human Rights and this means that all citizens of the UK are entitled to the following rights:

- life
- food
- liberty/free speech
- racial/sexual/religious equality
- education
- health care
- privacy.

In the UK today, these rights are protected by law. Most are covered by the Human Rights Act 1998 and anyone who feels that their rights have been infringed or abused can appeal to the European Court of Human Rights.

ResultsPlus
Watch out!

Some students think that human rights and Christian values are the same. Watch out! Although there are some similarities, there are also some important differences between them.

edexcel ::: key terms

Human rights – The rights and freedoms to which everyone is entitled.

The Human Rights Act includes important rights such as:

Everyone's right to life shall be protected by law.

No one shall be subjected to torture or inhuman treatment.

Everyone has the right to liberty (unless lawfully arrested and imprisoned).

Everyone charged with a criminal offence has the right to a fair trial.

Everyone has the right to a private family and home life.

Everyone has the right to freedom of expression and assembly (unless they are threatening national security or public safety).

Everyone has the right to live without prejudice.

Activities

1 Can you think of any real-life examples where human rights have been abused in the UK?

2 Imagine that you are a newspaper reporter who is interviewing a ruthless dictator who has abused human rights in their country. What questions would you ask?

Are human rights always right?

The law on human rights has done a lot to help those involved in child prostitution and illegal immigration. It has also been used in the UK to stop corporal punishment in schools and for equality for homosexuals.

The biggest area of controversy concerns national security and terrorism, where many believe that certain human rights should sometimes be overruled when national security is at risk. In other words, that suspected terrorists may not be entitled to human rights. However, others say that suspected terrorists should be entitled to human rights and that the Terrorism Acts of 2000 and 2006 abuse human rights by allowing the police to arrest and detain suspected terrorists for long periods of time. Between 2001 and 2007, 1,228 people were arrested on terrorism offences, of which 224 were convicted and imprisoned, 114 are awaiting trial and 890 were released without charge.

Activities

3 Do you think that national security should come before human rights? Explain your answer.

4 Do suspected terrorists have human rights?

Is the law correct?

Many people have criticised the Human Rights Act, claiming that sometimes it allows criminals to get away without proper punishment. Consider the following cases.

In 1996, a 15-year-old Italian student, Learco Chindamo, who was living in Britain, was found guilty of murdering his school headmaster, Philip Lawrence. The teenager was sentenced to 12 years' imprisonment, then he was to be sent back (deported) to Italy. However, he appealed and won the right to stay in the UK. Under the Human Rights Act, the court decided that he still had the right to 'family life' in the UK.

In 2006, nine Afghan men hijacked a Boeing 727 with 180 passengers on board and ordered the pilot to fly to the UK. The men were trying to escape the Taliban in their own country. The plane landed at Stansted Airport and the men were arrested. However, the court declared that, under the Human Rights Act, the men could stay in the UK, as to send them home to possible death was against their human rights.

For discussion

Do you agree or disagree with the decisions in the two cases above? Give your reasons.

Summary

- Human rights in the UK are legally created by Acts of Parliament.
- The government introduced measures such the Human Rights Act to prevent abuse of such rights.
- Today there are still problems enforcing human rights in difficult circumstances such as terrorism.

London in the aftermath of the bombings on 7 July 2005.

1.7 Why human rights are important to Christians

Learning outcomes

By the end of this lesson, you should be able to:

- describe the similarities between teachings in the Bible and human rights laws
- explain why human rights are important to Christians
- use examples of Christians who have worked to improve human rights
- express your own opinions on Christian attitudes to human rights.

edexcel **key terms**

The Decalogue – The Ten Commandments.

You shall not murder

You shall not commit adultery

You shall not steal

You shall not lie

Honour your mother and father

Some of the Ten Commandments.

Christians and human rights

Human rights are important to all Christians and all Christian Churches support the UN Declaration of Human Rights. Human rights are important to Christians because:

- Every human being is created by God, in God's image and all of God's creation should be treated with respect.
- God loves everyone equally so they should be treated equally.
- The teachings of the Bible are in line with most human rights laws.

The basic values and teachings of the Bible are summed up by the Ten Commandments (**the Decalogue**) (Exodus 20:2–17) and by the teachings of Jesus in the Sermon on the Mount (Matthew Chapters 5–7).

Christian values are the basis of many of the human rights provisions we have today.

Activities

1 Compare the Ten Commandments with the list of human rights. Which ones are the same and which ones are different? Why do you think this is?

The Bible and human rights

As well as the Ten Commandments and the Sermon on the Mount, there are many other teachings in the Bible that illustrate why human rights are important for Christians.

- The Parable of the Sheep and the Goats teaches that it is the moral duty of Christians to help people in need. '... *whatever you did for one of the least of these brothers of mine, you did for me*' (Matthew 25:40).
- Jesus said that the second most important commandment after loving God is '*Love your neighbour as you love yourself*' (Matthew 22:39).
- St Paul said: '*Remember those in prison as if you were their fellow prisoners, and those who are maltreated as if you yourselves were suffering*' (Hebrews 13:3).

What all of these teachings come down to is known as the Golden Rule (see page 20): '... *do to others what you would have them do to you ...*' (Matthew 7:12).

In the past, many famous Christians have worked to establish what we now call human rights. In the 19th century, the great Christian reformer, Lord Shaftsbury, campaigned against the awful working conditions in factories and the lack of education and health care for the children of poor families and William Wilberforce campaigned against the slave trade. Recently, Archbishop Desmond Tutu campaigned against racism and apartheid in South Africa.

Today, many Christians believe that it is important for the government to put human rights first. For example, they should spend money on things that do good for society, such as hospitals and schools and care for the poor and elderly. In the same way, some Christians campaign for the government to behave in a good and morally correct way, for example by making fair laws and condemning greed and promiscuity.

For discussion

'Christians should give all they have to the poor and needy.' Do you agree?

Activities

2 Can you think of any rights that Christians have that are not covered by human rights legislation?

3 Can you think of any human rights that are not in the Bible?

4 Create a poster of reasons why human rights are important to Christians.

Christians should be involved in helping to establish and protect human rights by helping the poor and suffering, working for world peace and for a fairer sharing of the world's resources.

Christians in a secular world

Of course, one of the major problems is that Christian teaching is concerned with loving God but society is run in a secular and not a religious way. Some Christians argue that, because of this, and because the UK is a multi-faith and multi-ethnic society, that Christian values should not be imposed upon the government and that Christians should stay out of political decisions.

Indeed, in the Bible, Paul tells Christians that they should obey political leaders because authority has been given to them by God. '*Everyone must submit himself to the governing authorities, for there is no authority except that which God has established. The authorities that exist have been established by God*' (Romans 13:1).

Summary

- Christians believe that human beings are created by God in God's image and have been given special rights.
- Many Christian principles have been used in human rights provision.
- There are still some differences between Christian values and human rights.

1.8 Why it is important to take part in democratic and electoral processes

Learning outcomes

By the end of this lesson, you should be able to:

- describe the way democracy works in the UK
- explain the basic views about democracy of the different political parties
- evaluate the importance of elections and taking part in the democratic process
- express your own opinions, giving reasons, as well as understand how they may differ from the opinions of others.

edexcel ⁙ key terms

Democratic processes – The ways in which citizens can take part in government (usually through elections).

Electoral processes – The ways in which voting is organised.

Political party – A group that tries to be elected into power on the basis of its policies, e.g. Labour, Conservative and Liberal Democrat.

Democracy in the UK

The word 'democracy' comes from the Greek *demos* (people) and *kratein* (rule). It is a political system, used in the UK and the Western world in which the ordinary people vote to decide who should represent them.

The UK is a representative democracy. This means that it is governed by an elected parliament. Every five years a general election is held where people vote for the **political party** that will form the next government. Participating in the **democratic process**, by voting, is important. The people that we vote for will be responsible for governing the country for the next few years and they will make important decisions affecting everyone's lives. For instance, the government makes decisions on how schools and colleges will be run, on the health service, on defence and on how much tax people should pay. Democracy means that everyone over 18 years old who is a British citizen has the opportunity to help to decide how the country is going to be run.

There are three main political parties in the UK, together with many smaller ones. In a general election, each party puts forward to the people its own views on what it would do if it were elected to power.

The Labour Party

The state should help the poor

The state should provide hospitals and schools for everyone equally

The Conservative Party

The state should encourage people to look after themselves

The state should only provide what people cannot pay for themselves

The Liberal Democrat Party

Green issues are important

The government and individuals should work together to help everyone

Some views of the main political parties in the UK.

Why is it important to vote?

Today, all British citizens over 18 years old can vote. This has not always been the case. Voting rights were restricted depending on gender, class and even whether you owned property. In the past, people considered the right to vote as extremely important – some were even prepared to die to try to win this right! This probably seems very strange and today in the UK the number of people who vote is quite low. So why do people think voting is so important?

Activities

1 Explain in your own words why voting is important.

Politics affects every single person in the UK. The policies and laws made by the national and local government rule our lives. They decide things like the taxes people will pay and how much money people will receive in benefits; how often our rubbish is collected; what health treatment people can get on the NHS; what human rights citizens are entitled to; whether the armed forces go to war – the list is endless. You may think that politics does not affect young people but you would be wrong – for example, the government decides what should be taught in schools.

The people we vote for will be responsible for these decisions and many more. This actually means that the voting public has a huge amount of political power. National and local governments are voted for because of their policies which they set out before elections take place. If the people who vote do not like what the government has done or is

doing, they have an opportunity to change this by voting for a different party at the next election.

Other ways of taking part

There are other ways in which citizens of Britain can take part in the democratic process.

- It is the job of the local Member of Parliament (MP) to represent people who live in his or her local area. You could write to your MP, or arrange an appointment to meet with them to speak about issues that you would like them to address.
- Lobbying means trying to influence decisions made by the government. This could be done in a variety of ways either privately, such as writing to MPs (as above) or publicly, such as taking part in a demonstration or signing a petition.
- People become members of political parties and work and campaign for them without necessarily wanting to become MPs themselves.

The ultimate way of taking part in the democratic processes in the UK is to stand for election yourself. Everyone who is allowed to vote is also allowed to stand for election, whether they are a member of a political party or not.

Activities

2 Write a leaflet explaining the different ways in which people can take part in the democratic and **electoral processes**.

3 Do you think Christians or other religious believers would agree that voting and taking part in the democratic process is important? Why/why not?

For discussion

'If you didn't vote, then you have no right to complain about what the government is doing.' Do you agree with this statement?

Summary

- Democracy in the UK is very important as it gives all citizens a say in who runs the country.
- People can take part in the democratic process and express their opinions in a variety of ways.

1.9 Christian teachings on moral duties and responsibilities

Learning outcomes

By the end of this lesson, you should be able to:

● explain the main Christian moral duties and responsibilities as set out in the Golden Rule, the parable of the sheep and the goats and 'My brother's keeper'

● how the Bible helps Christians to carry out their responsibilities

● express your own opinions on these teachings, giving reasons, as well as understand how they may differ from the opinions of others.

Christian moral duties and responsibilities

Christians believe that God makes moral commands, all of which are good, that they should follow. Being a Christian means living life according to God's moral code. The Bible teaches that all Christians have moral duties and responsibilities. The most well-known of these are the Ten Commandments (Exodus 20:2–17), some of which require believers to undertake the following moral duties:

● Honour your parents.
● Do not murder.
● Do not steal.
● Do not commit adultery.
● Do not lie.
● Do not covet other people's belongings.

In addition, in the Sermon on the Mount (Matthew Chapters 5–7) Jesus told his followers:

● To love their enemies
● to give to the needy
● not to store up treasure on Earth
● not to judge others.

Above all, Jesus gave what many Christians call **the Golden Rule**, that is, the guide to the way in which people must treat others. It teaches that all Christians, should '… *do to others what you would have them do to you…*' (Matthew 7:12). This means 'treat everyone how you would like them to be treated.'

edexcel key terms

The Golden Rule – Jesus' teaching that you should treat other people as you would like them to treat you.

Activities

1 Look at the biblical teachings opposite. Do you think they are (a) too hard to follow or (b) out of date? Say why or why not. Are there any other Christian values that ought to be on the list?

The sheep and the goats

Jesus' teaching on welfare is shown in the parable of the Sheep and the Goats (Matthew 25:31–46). He told the story of how God will, at the end, separate his people into those who have helped others (the sheep), and those who have not (the goats). Jesus taught that it is the moral duty of a Christian to feed those who are hungry, give clothes to the naked, give drink to the thirsty, visit the sick and help those who are in prison. If Christians do these things for people in need, then they are doing them for Jesus. '*I tell you the truth, whatever you did for one of the least of these brothers of mine, you did for me*' (Matthew 25:40).

Activities

2 **Role-play.** You are a Christian and your partner is (a) a prisoner and (b) a homeless person. In the light of Jesus' teaching, what would you say and do, and how would they respond?

For discussion

'Doing good deeds is never enough.' Do you agree?

'Christian moral teaching is fine in theory but impossible to carry out.' What do you think?

My brother's keeper

St Paul taught that Christians must not stand by while others are in need. Earlier, the Bible tells the story of Cain, a jealous man who killed his brother Abel. Cain then denied that he had anything to do with it and declared that it was not up to him to care for others. He asked, '*Am I my brother's keeper?*' (Genesis 4:9).

Paul uses this example to warn Christians that it is their moral duty actively to care for others. '*If anyone has material possessions and sees his brother in need but has no pity on him, how can the love of God be in him? … Let us not love with words or tongue, but with actions and in truth*' (II John 3:17–18).

Disabled people being cared for in 'Cheshire Home' which is part of an organisation run on Christian values to care for those in need.

Activities

3 How do the contrasting photographs fit in with the teaching of the Bible?

4 Imagine you are (a) one of the disabled people, and (b) President Clinton. How would you explain that you are both following Christian teachings?

5 Create an ideas map of all the Christian teachings on moral duties and responsibilities in the topic.

Summary

- Christians believe that God gives them moral duties and responsibilities.
- These are contained in the Bible such as the Golden Rule, the parable of the sheep and the goats, and my brother's keeper.
- Christianity stresses the importance of good works as well as faith in God.

The making of a peace agreement in 1993 between Israeli leader Rabin (left) and Palestinian leader Yasser Arafat (right), with US President Clinton in the middle.

1.10 The nature of genetic engineering

Learning outcomes

By the end of this lesson, you should be able to:

- explain the nature of genetic engineering, including cloning
- give some of the advantages and disadvantages of genetic engineering, and explain why it is controversial
- express your own opinions on genetic engineering, giving reasons, as well as understand how they may differ from the opinions of others.

What is genetic engineering?

Genes make up the DNA of every living thing. DNA is like a code or programme that determines what that organism will be like. For example, the genes you have inherited from your parents have determined the colour of your eyes. Genetic engineering is the process where the structure and characteristics of genes are changed. Simply put, this means that genes can be added, replaced or taken away, which means that genes that cause disorders can be removed or genes that cause 'improvements' can be added.

- Gene therapy is where cells are taken from an organism and grown in a laboratory where missing genes are inserted and the cells allowed to develop. Then these are put back into the bloodstream to cure genetic disorders.
- Genes can also be used to produce hormones and proteins. Examples of how this could be used are in the production of insulin, which would be of great help for sufferers of diabetes.
- Genes can be inserted so that animals can grow human parts (see the photo of the mouse opposite). This could have huge potential for people who need organ transplants.
- Genetic engineering could also be used to change the genes in an embryo. This could be used to get rid of inherited disorders such as cystic fibrosis.

Up to this point in time, most research on genetic engineering has been focused on plants and particularly the development of genetically modified (GM) crops.

Currently, the government have very strict control over the research and development of GM crops in the UK. Various types of GM crop plant have been grown and developed here, but only for research purposes but so far, they are not allowed to be grown and sold commercially. This is not the case in other parts of the world where farmers have been growing GM crops for some time.

The genetic engineering of plants opens up great possibilities such as growing crops that have better nutritional benefits; crops that are resistant to disease and pests, and crops that will grow in harsh climates or on unfertile land.

Activities

1 Study the photograph of the genetically engineered mouse below. What are the advantages of being able to do this? What are the disadvantages? Jot down your ideas.

This mouse has been genetically engineered to have a human ear on its back.

What is cloning?

A clone is an exact copy of something else. Reproductive cloning is a technology that is used to create an animal or plant with an identical genetic make-up to another. It is asexual reproduction – where a foetus is created from one person's or mammal's cells rather than two. Dolly the Sheep was the first successfully cloned mammal. Since then, many other species have been cloned. Cloning could have many uses. For example, it could be used to clone animals that were particularly good at something such as a brilliant racehorse or a cow that produces very high milk yields. It is currently illegal to clone human beings in the UK.

Another type of cloning is therapeutic cloning. This is the cloning of embryos to use in research on human development and disease. It is used to harvest stem cells. Stem cells are cells which are developed in an embryo to form many different cells in the body. Scientists are very excited about the possibilities of using these cells to produce other cells which could be used to cure illnesses such as Alzheimer's disease.

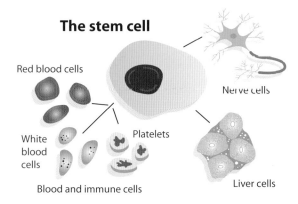

The stem cell

Red blood cells

Nerve cells

White blood cells

Platelets

Blood and immune cells

Liver cells

This diagram shows the different types of cells that stem cells could produce. Does this diagram help you to understand why scientists are so excited by stem cells?

Activities

2 In your own words, explain what genetic engineering and cloning are and how they could benefit people.

Some of the issues

Genetic engineering is a controversial subject. The growth and use of genetically modified plants has caused much debate in the UK. Even more controversial is the genetic engineering of animals and humans. Some of the arguments that people may raise against it are:

- Nature is very complex and nobody knows exactly what the effects might be. It is still early days in all of these developments and nobody yet knows whether GM crops, for example, can have a negative effect on the planet or on humans.
- In the wrong hands, these technologies could be very dangerous. For example, they could be used to mass-produce substances that could be used as biological weapons.
- Who decides what is defective and what is not? Maybe getting rid of genetic disadvantages is not such a good thing. It's part of what makes us all unique human beings.
- This could be the start of a slippery slope – it might eventually lead to 'designer babies'.

For discussion

How do you feel about the possibilities raised by the genetic engineering of plants and animals? Do they excite you? Do they scare you? Do you feel differently about the various types of genetic engineering?

'GM crops could potentially put an end to world hunger – it's got to be worth a try whatever the risks might be.' Discuss.

Summary

- Genetic engineering means changing the genetic make-up of a living organism.
- It has great potential for things like curing certain diseases or increasing crop yield.
- It is very controversial.

1.11 Christian attitudes to genetic engineering

24

'For it was you who created my inward parts; you knit me together in my mother's womb… My frame was not hidden from you when I was being made in secret, intricately woven in the depths of the Earth. Your eyes beheld my unformed substance. In your book were written all the days that were formed for me when none of them yet existed' (Psalm 139:13, 15–16).

As with many issues, there are different attitudes to genetic engineering in Christianity. However, all Christians believe that life is sacred and therefore, even those who agree with the many methods of genetic engineering believe that it should only be done for the right reasons such as healing the sick or feeding the hungry.

Reasons why Christians may accept genetic engineering

- Christians believe that God has given them *'dominion over the fish of the sea, the birds of the air, and every living thing that moves on the earth'* and some Christians would argue that includes the genes of these organisms. For these Christians, forms of genetic engineering, such as growing GM foods, would be acceptable as long as it did not cause harm.

- The Golden Rule of Jesus is to *'… do to others what you would have them do to you …'* (Matthew 7:12). For some Christians this would mean that genetic engineering is acceptable when it is for the cure of painful diseases and disorders.

- Jesus healed many people, which suggests that Christians should do all they can to heal and improve the health of human beings.

For discussion

'Whether you believe in God or not, it's dangerous to mess with nature.' Discuss your opinions on this statement.

Reasons why Christians may oppose genetic engineering

- Only God can create life and humans should not 'play at being God'. This is the most extreme view and Christians who believe this are likely to disagree with most types of genetic engineering, including things such as GM crops.

- Some Christians, such as Roman Catholics, believe that human life begins at the moment of conception and see an embryo as a 'person'. These Christians are opposed to anything that involves research on embryos which are then 'discarded', as they would see this as murder.

Activities

1 What types of genetic engineering are some Christians likely to agree with? Explain why.

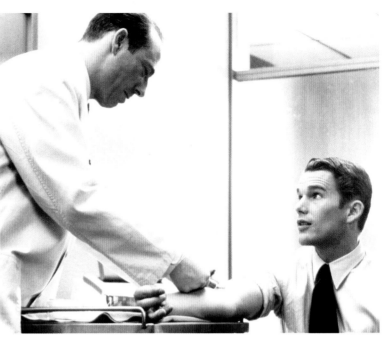

Vincent, the hero of Gattaca, *is an 'In-valid', which means that he is not genetically engineered. The society he lives in, treats In-valids as inferior people but Vincent defies the odds and manages to get a good job in a space agency by taking on the identity of a Valid person.*

Activities

2   How might these verses from Psalm 139 help a Christian to appreciate the picture above of an embryo in its mother's womb?

3   How might the meaning of the Psalm influence views about genetic engineering?

• Most Christians would be opposed to genetic engineering that corrects 'defects' which do not cause suffering, such as being short-sighted.

The vast majority of Christians are against the cloning of humans, not just because it is God's role to create life, but also because it takes away individuality and God makes each of us unique for a purpose. Christians would also be concerned about the effects that cloning would have on the person who has been cloned as well as the effects on society in general.

The film *Gattaca* (1997, Columbia Pictures) raises some important issues about what might happen if humans could 'design' their children. In the film, the best jobs and greatest respect can only be held by Valid people (who have been genetically engineered). People who are not engineered are called In-valids.

For discussion

In the film *Gattaca* the terms 'faith birth' and 'God child' are used to speak of non-engineered people.

What does this say to Christians about the spiritual dangers of genetic engineering?

The film uses a quotation from Ecclesiastes 7:13 as the title credits roll *'Consider God's handiwork; who can straighten what He has made crooked?'*

Discuss what this means about the relationship between God's creation and human involvement in making it a better place for humanity.

Summary

• Christians are divided in their views on genetic engineering.

• More liberal Christians see it as an opportunity to be involved in God's creative work and to help those who are sick and suffering.

• Conservative Christians are concerned that it may be 'playing God' and could be used for the wrong reasons.

exam zone

Know Zone
Rights and responsibilities

Quick quiz

1 What are the names given to the two main sections of the Bible?

2 Give an example of a moral law from the Bible.

3 Give an example of a moral law from the teaching of the Church.

4 Describe what Christians mean by conscience.

5 What does the parable of the Sheep and Goats teach about moral duties?

6 In what ways may Jesus be a moral role model for Christians?

7 Name three political parties in the UK.

8 What is cloning?

9 Why is genetic engineering controversial?

Plenary activity

In pairs, or as a group, choose one moral issue which may face an individual, for example, whether to have an abortion, or whether to fight in a war. Write this in the middle of a piece of A3 paper. Based on your studies in this section, make an ideas map of all the different methods the individual might use to help solve their dilemma. For example, they may refer to specific teaching in the Bible, or appeal to the law of the land. Make the map as detailed as possible, considering all moral authorities which may be taken into account. Once you have done this, suggest how they might decide which source of authority should be the most influential on their decision-making process.

Find out more

For more information on the following, go to www.heinemann.co.uk/hotlinks (express code 4233P) and click on the appropriate link.

- **UK human rights:** this is quite an unsophisticated website, but it identifies a whole range of areas in which some people feel that their rights are violated.

- **Ethics:** an excellent website that will help you with many issues in this section.

- **Moral Maze:** the website of the Radio 4 programme, which discusses moral issues and how they may be resolved.

- **Basic political rights in the UK:** use this website of the British Embassy in Israel to revise your knowledge of the basic political systems and rights processes in the UK.

Student tips

This is quite a varied section and some of it is tricky – I found learning about the electoral process and human rights more difficult, but fortunately, there is plenty of other material in the section to balance this out. You may need to spend more time revising the harder sections, though, because you have to accept that whatever question you choose to answer is likely to include one part on these areas.

Self-evaluation checklist

Read through the following list and evaluate how well you know and understand each of the topics.
How well have you understood the topics in this section? In the first column of the table below use the
following code to rate your understanding:

Green – I understand this fully

Orange – I am confident I can answer most questions on this

Red – I need to do a lot more work on this topic.

In the second and third columns you need to think about:

- Whether you have an opinion on this topic and could give reasons for that opinion if asked

- Whether you can give the opinion of someone who disagrees with you and give reasons for this alternative opinion.

Content covered	My understanding is red/orange/ green	Can I give my opinion?	Can I give an alternative opinion?
Why some Christians use only the Bible as a basis for making moral decisions.			
The authority of the Church for Christians and why some Christians use only the Church's teachings as a basis for making moral decisions.			
The role of conscience and why some Christians believe conscience is the most important guide when making moral decisions.			
Situation Ethics and why some Christians use only Situation Ethics as a guide when making moral decisions.			
Human rights in the UK.			
Why human rights are important for Christians.			
Why it is important to take part in democratic and electoral processes.			
Christian teachings on moral duties and responsibilities: the Golden Rule (Matthew 7:12), the parable of the Sheep and the Goats (Matthew 25:31–46), Am I my brother's keeper? (Genesis 4:1–10, 1 John 3:11–18).			
The nature of genetic engineering, including cloning.			
Different attitudes to genetic engineering and cloning in Christianity and the reasons for them?			

examzone

Know Zone
Rights and responsibilities

Introduction

In the exam you will see a choice of two questions on this section. Each question will include four tasks, which will test your knowledge, understanding and evaluation of the material covered. A 2-mark question will ask you to define a term; a 4-mark question will ask for your opinion on a point of view; an 8-mark question will ask you to explain a particular belief or idea; a 6-mark question will ask for your opinion on a point of view and ask you to consider an alternative point of view.

Here you need to give a short, accurate definition. You do not need to write more than one clear sentence.

You can give your opinion, but make sure you do give two clear and thought out reasons. These can be ones you have learned in class, even if they are not your own opinion. You shouldn't use terms such as 'rubbish' or 'stupid' as these don't show that you are able to think things through carefully.

Now you have to give the opposite point of view, again, using material you have learned during your studies. As before, give reasons you have learned in class. You must show you understand why people have these other views, even if you don't agree with them.

Mini exam paper

(a) What is the **Decalogue?**
(2 marks)

(b) Do you think it is important for Christians to take part in democratic processes?
Give **two** reasons for your point of view. (4 marks)

(c) Explain why some Christians agree with genetic engineering and some do not. (8 marks)

(d) 'Christians should always follow their conscience.'
In your answer you should refer to Christianity.
(i) Do you agree? Give reasons for your opinion. (3 marks)
(ii) Give reasons why some people may disagree with you. (3 marks)

Here you need to explain the reasons why some Christians support genetic engineering and others do not by showing you understand the reasoning behind these differences of opinion, not just listing the arguments for and against. This question is worth 8 marks so you must be prepared to spend some time answering it. You will also be assessed on your use of language in this question.

Again, you can use reasons you have learned from your studies, for or against. You need to give three simple reasons or fewer developed reasons.

Mark scheme

(a) You will earn 2 marks for a correct answer, and 1 mark for a partially correct answer.

(b) To earn up to the full 4 marks you need to give two reasons (as asked) and to develop them. Two brief reasons will earn 2 marks. One simple reason will only earn 1 mark.

(c) You can earn 7–8 marks by giving up to four reasons, but the fewer reasons you give, the more you must develop them. You are being assessed on your use of language, so you also need to take care to express your understanding in a clear style of English, and make some use of specialist vocabulary.

(d) To go beyond 3 marks for the whole of this question, you must refer to one religion. The more you are able to develop your answers, the fewer reasons you will need to give. Three simple reasons can earn you the same mark as one fully developed reason.

ResultsPlus
Maximise your marks

(b) Do you think it is important for Christians to take part in democratic processes?
Give **two** reasons for your point of view. (4 marks)

Student answer	Examiner comments	Improved student answer
I think there are several reasons why some may argue that Christians should not be involved in the democratic process. One is because the UK is not a religious society and so Christians should not try to push religious ideas onto a non-religious community because most people will not agree with Christian moral principles.	The candidate begins well by clearly stating their own beliefs on this issue. They then offer a brief reason for why they think this.	I think there are several reasons why some may argue that Christians should not be involved in the democratic process. One is because the UK is not a religious society and so Christians should not try to push religious ideas onto a non-religious community because most people will not agree with Christian moral principles.
Also, the UK is a multi-faith society.	Followed by another brief reason. This answer would receive 2 marks.	Also, the UK is a multi-faith society and it would be wrong for the democratic process to be seen to favour Christian views over those of other faiths.

Environmental and medical issues

Introduction

In this section you will learn about very important current issues relating to the environment and the beliefs of Christianity and Islam about stewardship of natural resources and the natural world. You will then move on to consider issues arising from medical treatments for infertility and organ transplantation, and religious views concerning them.

Learning outcomes for this section

By the end of this section you should be able to:

- give definitions of the key terms and use them in answers to GCSE questions
- outline the causes and possible solutions to global warming
- outline forms of pollution and possible solutions
- explain the scarcity of natural resources and how this poses a threat to the future of the planet, with possible solutions
- explain both Christian and Muslim teachings on stewardship and their effects on attitudes to the environment
- outline the nature and importance of medical treatments for infertility
- explain the different Christian and Muslim attitudes to infertility treatment
- outline the nature and importance of transplant surgery
- express your own opinions on the issues covered in this section and understand why some people hold views that are different from your own.

edexcel ::: key terms

artificial insemination	embryo	infertility	organ donation
conservation	environment	in-vitro fertilisation	stewardship
creation	global warming	natural resources	surrogacy

Fascinating fact

In the UK, 9,000 people need an organ transplant but only 3,000 people a year receive one. Around 1,000 people die waiting.

In pairs, take a sheet of A3 paper and write 'Environmental Issues' in the middle of the sheet. Then thought shower an ideas map identifying as many issues as you can that you think may relate to concern for the environment. As a starter issue, write 'Rubbish'. If you don't know why this is relevant, do some Internet research first, then move on to add your own ideas. Come back to this sheet at the end of the section to see if you had thought of everything you have covered!

This beautiful loch in Scotland is virtually undisturbed and is likely to remain so indefinitely.

For discussion

With your teacher, as a group, identify some natural areas you know which have been spoiled. Why has this happened? What would be needed to restore them? Do you think this is important? Is the loch attractive to you or does its remoteness make you feel uncomfortable?

2.1 Global warming

32

Learning outcomes

By the end of this lesson, you should be able to:

- explain what is meant by global warming
- explain the potential consequences and possible solutions
- express your own opinions about global warming, giving reasons, as well as understand how they may differ from the opinions of others.

What is global warming?

Since the middle of the 20th century the temperature of the Earth has been getting warmer. This is known as climate change or **global warming**.

Scientists have different opinions about why climate change is happening. However, many scientists think that recent climate change is being caused by humans – specifically, by burning fossil fuels (oil, coal and natural gas) which increases the levels of greenhouse gases such as carbon dioxide in the atmosphere. This stops some of the Sun's energy escaping and means that the temperature of the Earth is raised.

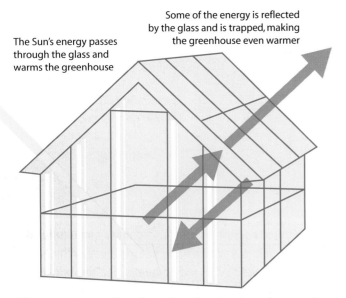

The Sun's energy passes through the glass and warms the greenhouse

Some of the energy is reflected by the glass and is trapped, making the greenhouse even warmer

The greenhouse effect describes the situation where carbon dioxide acts like the glass of a greenhouse. It allows the Sun's energy in, but does not allow it to get out. As a result, the temperature of the Earth rises because trapped heat cannot escape, and consequently, the climate changes.

edexcel ⠿ key terms

Global warming – The increase in the temperature of the Earth's atmosphere (thought to be caused by the greenhouse effect).

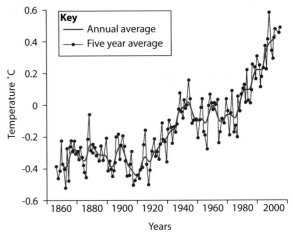

Graph showing the increase in global temperatures over the last 150 years. This tallies with the increasing use of fossil fuels.

Other scientists do not believe that greenhouse gases are the cause of global warming. They do not believe that the evidence is convincing. These scientists believe that the latest rises in temperature are a natural event. They would point out that the climate has always changed throughout the history of the Earth and this is just another one of those changes.

Activities

1 Explain what is meant by 'the greenhouse effect' in your own words.

2 Why do scientists disagree about the causes of global warming?

ResultsPlus
Watch out!

Some candidates get confused between the different environmental problems: global warming, pollution and lack of natural resources. Make sure that you know the difference between them.

What will happen?

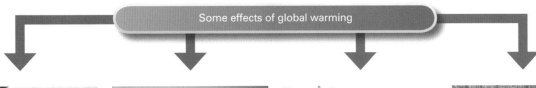
Some effects of global warming

As polar regions warm up, the ice melts, increasing the sea level. This means that many places are at risk of disappearing as the land will be underneath the sea.

As some places get hotter there will be more drought and, as other places get hotter, they will have more rain, leading to flooding. Both situations may lead to shortages of food and famine.

Extreme weather events such as hurricanes and flash floods will increase.

Some animals and plants will die out (become extinct) because they will not be able to adapt to the changing climate.

What can we do?

Obvious suggestions are to reduce the amount of energy being used and/or increase the use of 'clean' fuels to generate energy such as wind power, which does not produce greenhouse gases. There are many ways in which this can be done.

Action by individuals

All of us, especially in the most developed parts of the world, use large amounts of energy every day. Even small actions such as turning off electrical appliances when they're not being used or walking to the shops instead of using a car will help to reduce the amount of energy being used. Supporting environmental charities such as Greenpeace that lobby governments and fund scientific research is another way in which individuals can play a part.

Action by governments and international organisations

Most people believe that the only way we will be able to tackle climate change is if the whole world works together. There are many ways of doing this – for example, by setting laws that factories have to keep to in relation to the gases they produce. Many industrial countries have agreed to targets by which they have to reduce their greenhouse gas emissions. However, there is still a long way to go before all countries agree on both the causes and solutions of climate change.

Action by scientists

Scientific research is essential if humans are going to be able to tackle climate change. This means research into the causes and consequences of climate change – the more that we understand about why it is happening, the more able we will be to do something about it and research into possible solutions such as alternative energy sources or finding ways of reducing the amount of greenhouse gases in the atmosphere. However, all scientific research is very expensive.

Activities

3 In pairs, discuss the things you regularly do which use energy (for example, electricity, gas, fuel, etc). Think about how you might cut down on their use. What alternatives could you use?

Summary

Most scientists believe that global warming is caused by the greenhouse effect, the result of excessive levels of carbon dioxide being released into the atmosphere.

2.2 Pollution

Learning outcomes

By the end of this lesson, you should be able to:

- describe the main types of pollution and their causes
- explain some possible solutions
- express your own opinions on pollution.

Types of pollution

Pollution is the contamination of the environment, which damages and spoils it, so that it is no longer clean, healthy or able to provide the best possible conditions for humans or animals. Most pollution is caused by waste – products that humans do not want.

The problem of waste

Increased technology constantly leads to the development of new products which leads to a lot of waste, for example computers. Most waste cannot be recycled and is not biodegradable (it does not break down naturally if buried or exposed). Waste takes up space, spreads disease and releases dangerous chemicals into the environment, but we are generating more every year.

Land pollution

Land, or soil, pollution can lead to poor growth, loss of wildlife habitats, soil erosion, desertification and other types of pollution (such as water pollution). The most common example is dropping litter, but at industrial levels land pollution can be very serious. The most dangerous waste is radioactive waste. This can cause huge health problems for humans and other wildlife, as well as lowering soil fertility and stopping it growing food.

Other types of land pollution include deforestation (where forests are destroyed) and mining, both of which leave the land barren.

Air pollution

Air pollution happens when substances or chemicals affect the natural balance of the air. An example is sulphur dioxide and nitrous oxides from coal-fired power stations, which lead to acid rain. Acid rain harms soil, water and all forms of life as well as buildings. Air pollution can cause smog (industrial 'fog') and breathing problems for humans and animals. Many scientists believe that global warming is caused by air pollution (see pages 32–33).

Smoke from industry, and sometimes homes, pollutes the atmosphere and can cause respiratory illnesses such as asthma.

Water pollution

Water pollution is the contamination of rivers, lakes, oceans and reservoirs by chemicals or other matter that affects the water's quality.

Waste dumped at sea, usually sewage, oil or chemicals, affects land, rivers, animals, birds and ultimately humans.

One example of water pollution is eutrophication. This is when sewage and fertiliser make water plants grow. When they die, they are broken down by bacteria. As the bacteria feed, they use up the oxygen and the fish die.

Activities

1 Jot down some examples of land, air and water pollution and some ideas of the damage they might cause.

Thames 21 volunteers helping to clear out the river's banks.

Activities

2 Thames 21 is an organisation which helps to clean up the Thames as it runs through London. Rubbish is a common form of pollution and yet it should be one of the easiest to deal with. In pairs, or in a group, discuss and write down under different headings some suggestions for dealing with rubbish.

Possible solutions

Many people as individuals and organisations help to clean up pollution. See the picture of Thames 21 Volunteers above as an example. However, it would be far better to prevent the pollution from happening in the first place.

Create less waste

If there were less waste to dispose of, there would be less pollution. Individuals, businesses and governments can all play a part in creating less waste. Examples would be recycling things (using them again or sending things to recycling centres instead of putting them in rubbish bins) or buying products that have less packaging.

Government action

Many developed nations, such as the UK, have strict anti-pollution laws that help to limit pollution levels. They also impose severe penalties on companies that break these laws.

Alternative energy sources

Greater energy efficiency and using cleaner fuels that do not produce waste would mean there was less pollution (see pages 36–37).

Alternative manufacturing methods

Scientists are researching ways of manufacturing in ways that create less waste or that get rid of waste more effectively.

The ozone layer – a success story

In 1985 scientists discovered that there was a 'hole' in the ozone layer above the Antarctic. The ozone layer is the part of the atmosphere that prevents too much ultra-violet (UV) radiation entering the Earth. Too much UV exposure can cause many health problems for humans and animals, including skin cancer, and it also harms some crops and plants.

After researching into what was causing the problem, scientists found that certain man-made chemicals (CFCs) that are used in many fridges and spray cans were causing the destruction of the ozone layer. People were encouraged to stop using these products and in 1987 an international treaty was signed – the Montreal Protocol which agreed to limit the use of these chemicals.

The levels of CFCs in the atmosphere first levelled off before they started to reduce. Very slowly the ozone layer is beginning to repair itself.

Activities

3 Make a leaflet on at least one type of pollution. It should describe what is happening, explain what is causing the pollution and offer some possible solutions.

Summary

• Pollution is caused by human activity, industry, waste and negligence.

• The effects of pollution are very serious, affecting the world for both humans and wildlife.

2.3 Natural resources

Learning outcomes

By the end of this lesson, you should be able to:

● understand the importance of natural resources

● explain why conserving natural resources is important

● express your own opinions on the use of natural resources.

edexcel ⠿ key terms

Conservation – Protecting and preserving natural resources and the environment.

Natural resources – Naturally occurring materials, such as oil and fertile land, which can be used by humans.

Natural resources are provided by nature and can be used by humans. There are two types of natural resources:

Renewable resources

These are resources which replace themselves or can be replaced by humans. Examples are:

● wind power
● solar power (from the Sun)
● wave power
● water power
● fertile land
● wood.

Some of these resources need managing to be renewable. For example, land needs to be looked after to stay fertile and trees need to be planted to replace the ones used. However, these resources have great advantages for humans because they will never run out. Most of them are also 'clean' energy, which means they do not cause pollution. However, they have disadvantages too.

A wind farm in the UK.

Many of them are only effective in certain places (not everywhere gets much sunlight, for example) and they can also be more financially expensive than other resources.

Non-renewable resources

Non-renewable resources cannot be replaced once they are taken from the environment; once we have used them up, they will be gone forever. These include:

● coal
● oil
● gas
● minerals and rocks (such as iron ore).

Some of the resources (such as metals) can be recycled, which means that people can use them over and over again. Many of them cannot be recycled.

Humans use non-renewable resources for many different things:

● Transport – most vehicles run on petrol or diesel, which come from oil.
● Electricity – the vast majority is generated from non-renewable sources. These provide power for people's homes and businesses.
● Buildings – things like glass, bricks and steel which make our homes and places of work and entertainment are all made from minerals.
● Products – a huge number of products are made wholly or partly from non-renewable resources. These include things like cosmetics, DVDs, medicines and some foods.

What happens when the resources run out?

By now you will be getting the idea that humans are currently very reliant on non-renewable resources. Whether it happens in a few years or a few hundred years, if humans continue to use these resources as they are at the moment, they will run out. Current estimates suggest that oil reserves may run out within fifty years.

This will have an enormous impact and severe consequences on humans and life as we know it. It will affect all parts of life. For example, think about the way that most people in the world get their food. Agriculture, manufacturing, transport and the retail industries are all heavily dependent on non-renewable resources.

What can we do?

There are many different ways in which we can help.

Conservation is concerned with preserving the Earth's natural resources. This means looking after the environment so that future generations can enjoy it. People also need to make greater use of renewable resources and invest in developing other renewable sources of energy. Individuals can make a difference. Some ideas are:

● not wasting electricity – for example, by not leaving lights, computers or the television switched on

● walking, cycling or using public transport instead of driving the car
● buying and using products made from renewable resources.

There are millions of cars in the UK, all of which add to air pollution and make use of valuable non-renewable resources.

Summary

● Non-renewable resources are natural resources such as coal and gas which will eventually run out.

● Renewable resources are natural resources which renew themselves such as wind and the Sun, which can be used to generate power.

● Natural resources are often wasted and misused with serious long-term effects on the environment and on the quality of life for everyone.

2.4 Christian teaching on stewardship and attitudes to the environment

Learning outcomes

By the end of this lesson, you should be able to:

● explain Christian teachings on stewardship

● explain how these teachings affect Christian attitudes to the environment

● express your own views on these Christian teachings.

edexcel ⠿ key terms

Creation – The act of creating the universe or the universe which has been created.

Environment – The surroundings in which plants and animals live and on which they depend to live.

Stewardship – Looking after something so it can be passed on to the next generation.

Christian teachings

Three are three concepts at the heart of Christian teachings on the **environment**:

> **STEWARDSHIP: care for the environment and its resources**

> **RESPONSIBILITY: recognising that it is up to people to care for the natural world**

> **AUTHORITY OR DOMINION: having a position of power or headship over the natural world**

Hastings Country Park, Covehurst Bay.

Activities

1 Should Christian concern for stewarding the environment be focused on areas which can be used for growing crops? What is the point of stewarding an area of natural beauty such as the Hastings Country Park shown above? Why might some Christians argue that this is not what God meant in Genesis 2?

In the biblical account of **creation** it says

'God blessed them, and said to them "Be fruitful and multiply. Rule over the fish of the sea and the birds of the air and over every living thing that moves on the ground"' (Genesis 1:28).

This means that Christians believe that God has given humans the right to rule over the rest of the Earth (dominion). However, they also have a responsibility to care for God's creation. In fact, after God created the world, the Bible says that he asked mankind to *'till the earth and keep it'* (Genesis 2:15).

Most Christians would argue that people should look after the Earth and conserve natural resources because:

● All Christians believe that after death they will be judged by God for their actions while they were living. Most Christians believe that this includes how they have looked after the Earth.

- The Bible shows God's anger towards people who have ruined the environment: *'I brought them into a fertile land to eat its fruit and its produce. They came and made my land unclean. They made my property disgusting'* (Jeremiah 2:7).
- Jesus' teachings on loving one another and helping people in need mean that Christians today should share the resources of the world more equally.

Activities

2 'If God has given people authority over the Earth, doesn't that mean we can do what we like with it?' Write a response which most Christians would give to this question.

3 Are Christian teachings on the environment similar or different from your own views? Explain your answer.

4 In what ways does this photograph show a failure in Christian stewardship? As a group, discuss what other factors lead to this kind of natural and human devastation. Could more focus on religion help to solve these problems?

Careless attitudes towards the environment can have devastating effects.

- The idea at the heart of Christian **stewardship** is to look after the resources of the Earth for future generations: *'A good man leaves an inheritance for his children's children'* (Proverbs 13:22).

What does this mean in practice?

The teachings above suggest that Christians should try to:

- conserve the Earth's natural resources
- reduce pollution
- share the Earth's resources more equally across different parts of the world
- conserve animals and plant life.

People and God's creation

Christians are concerned to see that it is God, not nature that is worshipped. The environment is a gift from God and not something holy in itself. Christians believe that people are the most important part of God's creation, and so although conservation of the environment is of vital concern, it should not be at the expense of people or carried out for purely political purposes.

For discussion

How can environmental groups make their knowledge appealing to religious believers?

Summary

- Christians believe that the Earth was created by God and that he wants humans to look after it as stewards.
- Christians therefore try to look after the Earth and conserve natural resources, but believe that people are the most important part of the Earth.

2.5 Muslim teaching on stewardship and attitudes to the environment

> **Learning outcomes**
>
> By the end of this lesson, you should be able to:
> - understand Muslim teachings on stewardship
> - explain how these teachings affect Muslim attitudes to the environment
> - express your own views on these Muslim teachings.

Muslim teachings on the environment

Like Christians, Muslims believe that God created the world. Indeed, they believe the world is Allah's gift to mankind.

Islam teaches that Adam, the first human, was made as a khalifah or vice-regent over the Earth: *'It is he who has made you custodian, inheritors of the Earth'* (Surah 6:165). This means that humans were put in charge of the rest of God's creation. However, it does not mean they can do what they like with it. Instead Muslims believe:

- People should treat their gift from Allah (the Earth) with respect and look after it.

- As khalifah, humans have been placed in a position of responsibility to care for the world in the way that Allah wishes.

- All the different pieces of Allah's creation are in unity with each other. Therefore, everything is dependent on everything else and the balance has to be maintained for things to keep working as they should do:

> *'The sun and moon follow courses exactly computed; and the herbs and the trees – both alike bow in adoration. And the firmament he has raised high, and he has set up the balance in order that you may not transgress that balance'* (Surah 55:5–8).

- All Muslims are part of the ummah (Muslim brotherhood). This includes past and future generations of Muslims as well as those living all over the world today. Therefore, all members of the ummah should share in the Earth's resources, which means looking after the environment for the future. It also means that natural resources should be shared more equally between people today.

- Animals are part of Allah's creation and as his khalifahs, humans should therefore treat them with respect.

- On the Day of Judgement, Allah will judge everyone according to how they have lived their lives and carried out his wishes. This includes judging people on whether they have behaved as 'stewards of the Earth' should do.

In 1986, representatives of conservation agencies and world religions met at Assisi to discuss environ-mental concerns. The Muslim representatives observed: *'Allah's trustees [all Muslims] are responsible for maintaining the unity of his creation, the integrity of the Earth, its flora and fauna, its wildlife and its natural environment.'*

Activities

1 Compare Muslim and Christian teachings on stewardship and the environment. What teachings do they share? What are the differences? You may find it helpful to use a table to compare them.

What does this mean for the environment?

Some of the ways in which Muslims may put the teachings on the environment into practice are:

- to avoid extravagant or greedy use of resources
- not to damage, destroy or abuse the natural environment

Muslim conservationists at work.

- to work towards the protection and conservation of all existing forms of life
- to try to distribute the Earth's resources more equally
- to support environmental organisations and charities.

To fulfil their task as vice-regents over creation, Muslims should be aware of how they affect the environment positively and negatively, avoiding waste and pollution, using recycled and biodegradable products, and reducing energy use. Planting trees and crops, taking care of them and using them for the good of others will be blessed by Allah.

For discussion

'Religious believers should be leading the world in finding solutions to environmental problems.' Discuss.

Activities

2 Using what you have learned about Muslim teachings on the environment, how do you think Muslims would approach some of the environmental problems at the start of this section (pollution, global warming and a shortage of natural resources)? Explain your reasons.

Results Plus
Exam question report

Choose **one** religion other than Christianity and explain why followers should look after the environment. (8 marks)

How students answered:

Many candidates scored poorly on this question because their answers were generally about environmental problems and how people should respond, rather than focusing on religious responses.

Some candidates wrote good answers that gave a few examples of how believers from one religion respond to environmental issues. Generally, answers at this level did not give enough detail on the religious teachings.

There were some excellent and thoughtful answers that gave a detailed response explaining teachings on the environment in the religion, with examples of how followers of a religion cared for the environment.

Summary

- Muslims teach that Allah gave humans authority over creation, and they are his vice-regents on Earth, with the responsibility of stewardship.
- Everything in creation glorifies Allah and is part of the magnificence of his work, and should therefore be treated with respect.

2.6 Medical treatment for infertility

Learning outcomes

By the end of this lesson, you should be able to:

- describe the main fertility treatments available
- explain why these may be controversial
- express your own opinions, giving reasons, as well as understand how they may differ from the opinions of others.

edexcel ::: key terms

Artificial insemination – Injecting semen into the uterus by artificial means.

Embryo – A fertilised egg in the first eight weeks after conception.

Infertility – Not being able to have children.

In-vitro fertilisation – The method of fertilising a human egg in a test tube.

Surrogacy – An arrangement whereby a woman bears a child on behalf of another woman.

Infertility

To be infertile means being unable to have a baby naturally. Up to 10 per cent of couples in the UK who want to have children suffer from problems of **infertility** and for many of them it brings great emotional pain.

There are a wide range of medical treatments for infertility now available. These either use the sperm and egg of the parents or the sperm and/or egg which have been donated by another person.

Activities

1 Create a grid of three columns of all the fertility treatments listed opposite. In the second column write your own explanation of what the treatment involves.

Artificial insemination *by donor (AID)* The sperm of a donor, usually unknown to the couple, is medically inseminated into the mother's womb.

Artificial insemination by husband/partner (AIH) The partner's sperm is medically inseminated into the mother's womb.

Egg donation The partner's sperm is used to fertilise the egg of an unknown donor female in a test-tube, before being placed in the woman's womb.

Embryo *donation* Both sperm and egg are provided by anonymous donors, fertilised in a test-tube and then placed in the woman's womb.

In-vitro fertilisation *(IVF)* An egg is taken from the mother and fertilised in a test-tube using sperm from her partner or a donor, and then placed in her womb where she carries it to full term.

Surrogacy Egg, sperm, or both, of the couple are fertilised in a test tube and then placed in the womb of another woman who carries the baby to full term before handing it over to the couple.

Some problems

- Fertility treatments are very expensive, whether for the couples themselves or for the National Health Service (not all treatments are available on the NHS).
- There are no guarantees that fertility treatment will work and many attempts over several years may be needed.
- Fertility drugs can cause uncomfortable side-effects.
- It places the individuals and their relationship under huge amounts of strain.
- Having a baby through using donor sperm or a donor egg can be very difficult for the infertile partner to come to terms with and may lead to problems bonding with a baby who is not their own biological child.

Perhaps the hardest situation to cope with is surrogacy. The surrogate may find it difficult to give up a baby that she has carried for nine months and the couple may feel distant from the baby or feel that they are not in control of the situation.

Is it right?

All infertility treatment raises some ethical questions:

Is it right for the NHS to spend hundreds of thousands of pounds on fertility treatments when that money could be spent on treating people with life-threatening conditions and illnesses?

Is it ever right to interfere with nature at all?

The world is already very over-populated. Isn't being unable to have children nature's way of trying to control population levels?

Who is entitled to this treatment? Married couples? Unmarried couples? Same-sex couples? Single people? Who has the right to decide?

There are many unwanted or orphaned children in the world. Would adopting a child not be a better solution?

For discussion

Everyone has the right to their own biological child.

Specific treatments are also controversial, particularly those that use donors:

- Is it right that sperm and egg donors are not responsible for the children conceived?
- Should children always have the right to know their biological parents?

Surrogacy is possibly the most controversial of all fertility treatments because there is a debate about who is the 'real mother' of the child.

Activities

2 In the third column of the table you created in the first activity, write down some of the reasons why the treatment might be controversial. Remember to include your own ideas as well as those mentioned here.

3 What answers would you give to some of the ethical questions in the speech bubbles on the left? Select at least three and write down your own opinions. Remember to give your reasons why you think this.

4 Should fertility treatments be available to same-sex couples who wish to donate sperm or eggs, or use a surrogate? Discuss whether you think same-sex couples should have the right to the same treatment in this area as heterosexual couples. Remember this is a difficult issue, because your answers shouldn't be based on prejudice but on what is fair and right.

A same-sex couple with their child.

Summary

- Infertility (the inability to conceive a child naturally) causes problems and emotional suffering for many couples.
- There are several medical treatments available for infertility, all of which are controversial, but which bring great benefits to many couples.

2.7 Christian attitudes to medical treatment for infertility

Learning outcomes

By the end of this lesson, you should be able to:

● explain different Christian attitudes to infertility treatment

● give your own opinions on different Christian views.

For discussion

Why do you think that some Christians feel 'ashamed' that they cannot naturally have a child? How might they be helped to deal with this feeling?

Childless couples

Childlessness is a major problem for some Christian couples who believe that if they cannot have a child they are not able to fulfil God's command to humans to *'be fruitful and multiply'* (Genesis 1:28).

This book cover includes the subtitle 'Living With The Secret Shame of Infertility'.

Christian couples may respond in a variety of ways to not being able to have children:

● Some may accept that it is God's choice for them not to have children.

● Some may find other ways to direct their parental skills such as school, charity or church work.

● Some may choose to adopt children and therefore give unwanted or orphaned children a loving home.

● Some may choose to try to conceive a child through fertility treatment.

Christians who are against fertility treatments

Christians are divided over the use of artificial methods to have children. Some Christians, such as Roman Catholics, are opposed to all fertility treatments because they believe:

● God intended that children should be created through the natural act of sex between a husband and wife.

● No one has a 'right' to have children. God has a plan for everyone and if it is within his plan for a couple not to have a child, then people should respect that.

● Masturbation is a sin and all treatments where fertilisation takes place outside the woman's body involves masturbation by the male.

'Techniques which allow someone other than the husband and wife to be involved in the making of a child are very wrong. Techniques which separate sex from the making of the baby are unacceptable.'
(The Catechism of the Catholic Church)

Some Christians have objections to particular fertility treatments:

● Some Christians, including Catholics, are opposed to IVF because it involves the creation of several embryos. The embryos that are not used are destroyed and some are experimented on, which can be seen as violating the 'sanctity of life'.

● Many Christians would object to treatments which use donated sperm or eggs because they believe this would be adultery.

• Most Christians do not agree with surrogacy because it involves a third person, which may cause complications for all involved.

> *'In surrogacy, even if both sperm and ovum are contributed by the married couple, a physical and emotional bonding takes place between the 'mother' and the child she is carrying, which may later be hard to break.'*
> (John Stott, Issues Facing Christians Today)

Activities

1 Look back to the list of fertility treatments on page 42 and the grids that you created about them. Create another grid of four columns with each treatment in the first column. Put a heading 'Reasons why Christians may disagree with this treatment' at the top of the second column and fill it in. Some reasons will apply to all treatments whereas others will only apply to some.

Christians who agree with fertility treatments

Few Christians would agree with all types of fertility treatments for the reasons mentioned above. However, many would accept them in cases where the sperm of the husband and the egg of the wife are used (in IVF or AIH) because they believe that:

• God has given humans the capacity to create children in this way.
• It allows couples to experience the joy of having children.
• It is a way of loving your neighbour and follows the Golden Rule.

Activities

2 Add a heading to the third column of your grid: 'Reasons why Christians may agree with this treatment' and fill it in.

3 In the final column, fill in your own views about Christian reasons for agreeing and disagreeing with each type of treatment.

Other issues

Even if Christians agree with some fertility treatments, for many Christians it would depend upon the situation. Some would only agree with it for childless couples who are married. Some Christians may disagree with it for couples who already have children but want more. Many Christians would be concerned about using fertility treatment to enable same-sex couples to have children.

45

For many Christians, two children is the ideal number, whereas for others two might not be enough. Some Christians would not agree with the use of fertility treatment in these cases.

Summary

• Christians are divided about fertility treatment as some believe that only natural means of conception should be used because of the problems which may arise.
• Others believe that God has given humans the chance to develop fertility treatments so they are allowed.

2.8 Muslim attitudes to medical treatment for infertility

Commitment to family

All Muslims are expected to have children as they believe that this is what Allah wants. Infertility can be very painful for Muslim couples who may feel that they are not carrying out Allah's will. Therefore, most Muslims believe that help should be given to couples who cannot have children naturally. Some types of fertility treatment are allowed because:

- infertility is regarded as a disease so it is OK to try to find a cure
- they view childbirth and child-rearing as important family commitments
- having children helps to keep the couple and the family together
- the social status of the Muslim woman, her self-esteem and her place in the family and society as a whole are closely related to her ability to have a child.

IVF and AIH are permitted in Islam because:

- They use the sperm and egg of the married couple
- God has given people the ability to create life in this way
- Embryos that are destroyed during IVF are 14 days old so they are not classed as 'human'. Islam teaches that the soul does not enter the foetus until 120 days.

There is no guarantee that fertility treatment will work, of course, but if not, that is the will of Allah:

'To God belongs the dominion of heavens and earth. He creates what He wills. He bestows female (offspring) upon whom He wills, and bestows male (offspring) upon whom He wills. Or He bestows both males and females, and He leaves barren whom He wills. For He is All-Knowledgeable All-Powerful.' (Surah 42:49–50)

For discussion

The importance of the family within Islam justifies fertility treatment. Why do you think the family is seen as so valuable within Islam?

What is not allowed?

Some Muslims may take the teachings of the Qur'an (see quotation above) to mean that if it is the will of Allah for a couple not to have a child, then the couple should accept it and not have any type of artificial treatment.

The family is at the heart of Islam and all Muslims are expected to have children.

Most Muslims disagree with any treatment that uses donor sperm or donor eggs because:

- this is seen as adultery or violating the contract of marriage. Divorce or death brings a marriage contract to an end and for this reason a woman may not use the sperm of her former husband to conceive.
- Muslims believe that all children have the right to know their natural parents.

Surrogacy is banned in Islam for several reasons. First, because it is seen as violating the marriage contract and secondly, because it is considered that the woman who gives birth to a baby is the mother.

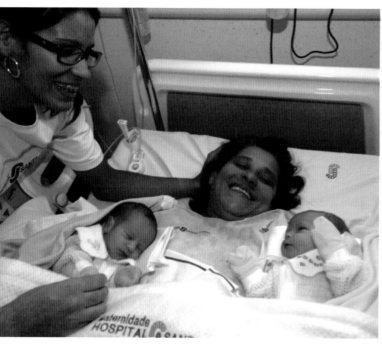
A 51-year-old gave birth to her daughter's twins in Brazil. Brazilian law stipulates that only close relatives can serve as surrogate mothers.

Activities

1 Look back at the list of fertility treatments on page 42. Sort them into two categories of treatments that most Muslims would agree with and those that most Muslims would disagree with. For each one, explain in a short sentence the reasons why Muslims agree or disagree with the treatment.

Activities

2 What do you think? Now that you have found out about fertility treatments and Christian and Muslim attitudes towards them, write down your own opinions and explain your reasons. Do you have a general view about all treatments or do you have a different view for different treatments?

ResultsPlus
Build better answers

Do you think that it is right for childless couples to use fertility treatment?
Give **two** reasons for your point of view. (4 marks)

■ **Basic, 1-mark answers**
These answers will offer their view with one brief reason.

● **Good, 2–3-mark answers**
Answers that receive 2 marks will give their view and support it with a developed reason or will give two brief reasons. For one brief reason and one developed reason, 3 marks will be awarded.

▲ **Excellent, 4-mark answers**
To gain full marks, candidates need to give their view and support it with two developed reasons.

Summary

- Because the family is of such importance to Islam, and childbearing to a woman's self-esteem and status, fertility treatment is permitted within certain limits.
- Fertility treatment must not break or violate the marriage bond.

47

2.9 Transplant surgery

Learning outcomes

By the end of this lesson, you should be able to:

● describe transplant surgery and organ donation

● explain some of the advantages and problems associated with organ donation.

edexcel ▦ key terms

Organ donation – Giving organs to be used in transplant surgery.

A UK donor card is voluntary and indicates that the carrier of the card would like their organs to be used for transplantation after their death.

What is transplant surgery?

Transplant surgery involves using body parts from one person, dead or alive, to replace body parts in someone else. The most common transplants are: kidney, liver, lungs, heart and heart valves, corneas, blood and bone marrow, tissues, pancreas.

Transplant surgery is an established and advanced form of treatment but which, despite its potential to do enormous good, raises many ethical problems. On the plus side:

● Organ transplants make use of organs which would otherwise be wasted.
● It gives people and their loved ones the opportunity to help others after their death.
● It offers tremendous relief and is an enormous blessing both to those who receive transplants and to their loved ones.

On the minus side:

● It is a very expensive and limited form of treatment.
● It raises important questions about when a person is actually dead.
● Should a person be kept alive or allowed to die purely for the purposes of organ donation?
● Donor organs are very scarce and in some countries a black market in organs has developed.

For discussion

Do you think that it should be compulsory to carry a donor card? Should loved ones have the right to refuse donation to go ahead?

Organ donation

Most donated organs come from dead donors. This raises problems as it may be seen to conflict with offering the best available care to the donor patient. Loved ones may feel pressured to make a quick decision about donating the organ of a dying person when they may not yet even be ready to accept that the patient is going to die.

In the UK, **organ donation** is voluntary and willingness to donate organs is shown by an organ donation card. However, in some countries people must opt out of organ donation otherwise healthy organs can be used for transplantation and relatives cannot challenge this. One person's organs can give life to up to seven different people!

'All religious people should carry a donor card.'
In your answer you should refer to at least
one religion.
(i) Do you agree? Give reasons for your opinions.
     (3 marks)
(ii) Give reasons why some people may disagree
     with you. (3 marks)

■ **Basic, 2-mark answers**
For part (i), answers would be given 1 mark for
giving one simple reason for their opinion. For part
(ii), answers would be given 1 mark for giving one
simple reason why others may disagree with them.

● **Good, 4-mark answers**
Answers would be given 2 marks for both parts if
they offer two simple reasons or one developed
reason. Answers cannot gain more than 3 marks in
total if the opinions of believers from one religion
have not been included.

▲ **Excellent, 6-mark answers**
To gain full marks for both parts, answers need
to give three simple reasons or two developed
reasons or one fully developed reason for both
parts (i) and (ii).

Activity

1 The shortage of donor organs has led many
   people, particularly in the USA, to advertise for a
   live donor.

   To see some examples of ads for live donors, go
   to www.heinemann.co.uk/hotlinks (express code
   4233P): live donor ads.

   Do you think these are a good way of finding
   donors? What are the problems?

For some transplants it is not necessary for the
donor to be dead. This is the case with liver, kidney
and bone marrow transplants. In the UK, only
genetically related live donors can be used, since the
motivations of those donating organs are otherwise
difficult to monitor. It is illegal in the UK to use
organs donated as part of a commercial transaction.

Non-religious problems of organ donation

One of the major problems facing medical teams
making decisions about organ donation is the
question of who gets the organ. Should it be:

* the person who has been on the waiting list for a
  transplant the longest
* or the person with the best tissue match, and
  therefore the least chance of rejecting the organ
* or the youngest person?

Another problem is the prospect of xenografting
(using organs from animals). Animal organs may
carry diseases which would affect humans. Many
people have concerns about using animals in
this way.

Summary

* Transplant surgery involves replacing defective
  organs with healthy ones from a dead or
  live donor.
* People can volunteer to be organ donors before
  their death, or their loved ones can make that
  choice if they have not carried a donor card.
* Organ donation is a gift of life to someone who is
  almost certainly going to die.
* There are many problems associated with organ
  donation including scarcity of organs and whether
  people should be allowed to advertise for a donor.

2.10 Christian attitudes to transplant surgery

Learning outcomes

By the end of this lesson, you should be able to:

● explain why most Christians agree with transplant surgery with certain conditions

● explain why some Christians disagree with transplant surgery

● give your own opinions on Christian attitudes to transplant surgery.

Christian views

For most Christians there are no moral problems with donating an organ because:

● It is a loving and charitable act which fulfils Jesus' teaching to love one another.

● It raises no problems for life after death, since a body will not be needed in heaven.

● It is a way in which people can show their gratitude for God's gift of life.

Most Protestant Churches teach that organ donation is a matter of personal conscience and each person should make their own decision about it. The Roman Catholic Church teaches that transplant surgery is a very positive thing and encourages people to become organ donors.

However, Christians naturally have some concerns about this difficult procedure. The donation of organs should be done in a responsible way which reflects loving charity. The Roman Catholic publication, *The Ethical and Religious Directives for Catholic Health Care Services*, produced by the National Conference of Catholic Bishops, lays out a set of principles.

Activities

1 What does the quotation from the *Religious Directives* mean? Discuss it as a group with your teacher. What does 'conflict of interest' mean and why might there be a conflict of interest in these matters? What special interest has the transplant team in determining whether a patient has died?

'Such organs should not be removed until it has been medically determined that the patient has died. In order to prevent any conflict of interest, the physician who determines death should not be a member of the transplant team.'
The Ethical and Religious Directives for Catholic Health Care Services

The *Directives* also outlines the view that the decision as to who receives organs should be made on medical grounds and not be based on age, sex or social status.

Pope John Paul II observed in *Evangelium Vitae*:

'There is an everyday heroism, made up of gestures and sharing, big or small… A particularly praiseworthy example of such gestures is the donation of organs in a morally acceptable manner'.

For discussion

Is organ donation a heroic thing? If so, who is the hero: the patient who has died or the loved ones who are prepared to allow the organs of the dead person to be given?

Is it equally brave if someone who is alive and well donates an organ or bone marrow in order to help someone else to live?

Why some Christians disagree

Although most Christians agree with transplant surgery provided that it is done in a certain way, some Christians are opposed to it. This is because they believe:

- It violates the sanctity of life and people should not 'play God'.
- The organs are an essential part of an individual which God has created and it would be wrong to replace part of that person.
- Transplant surgery is interfering with God's plans for each individual.

Christian views may also depend on the reason why a person's organs need replacing. Some Christians may disagree with replacing an organ if it is necessary because the person had abused their body which God had created. An example might be someone who has destroyed their liver because they would not stop drinking alcohol.

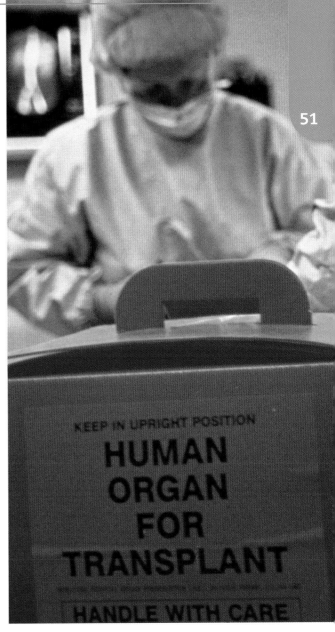

An organ cooler in an operating room during an organ transplant.

Activities

2 In pairs, discuss how a Christian may feel about organ donation in these situations:

   (a) A child has died in a road accident and another child can be saved by receiving their heart.

   (b) A family man in his 40s dies suddenly and his liver is used to save the life of an older man suffering from alcohol-induced liver damage.

   (c) An elderly woman is told that she is too old to receive a kidney transplant from the usual means, so her granddaughter offers one of her kidneys.

3 Which Christian view is most like your own opinion? Explain your answer.

4 Write an article entitled 'Christian views on transplant surgery' for a magazine. Remember to include all views.

For discussion

What do you think is happening in the photograph? How does it make you feel?

Is there anything about it which may disturb Christians?

Summary

- Most Christians are positive about organ donation, believing it to be a chance to share in God's gift of life.
- Although a few Christians may be opposed to it, most see it as an act of love and charity which should be encouraged.

51

2.11 Muslim attitudes to transplant surgery

Learning outcomes

By the end of this lesson, you should be able to:

- explain Muslim teaching on organ transplantation
- express your own opinions, giving reasons, as well as understand how they may differ from the opinions of others.

Muslim views

Islam, like the other main world religions, believes that organ donation is an individual choice. However, many Muslims believe that transplanting an organ from a dead person into another person is wrong because:

- The Qur'an teaches that the body should not be interfered with after death and should be buried as soon as possible.
- Muslims believe that on the Last Day, the body will be resurrected and therefore all the organs will be needed.
- It violates the sanctity of life – only Allah has the right to give life and take it away.

Some Muslims would also disagree with transplanting organs from living donors for similar reasons. However, this is less controversial because organs that can be transplanted from living people are not essential (for example, people can survive with one kidney). This means it would not affect the resurrection of the body. Therefore, many Muslims would allow living donor transplants if the donor was a close relative.

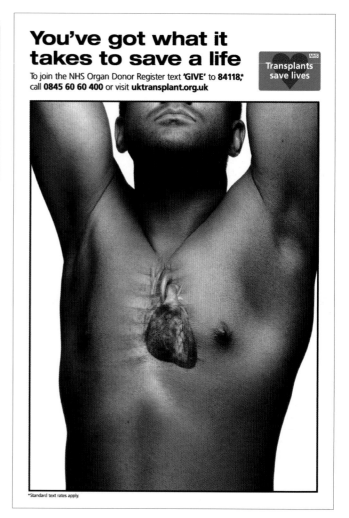

A poster for organ donation.

Other Muslims agree with organ transplants from the dead as well as the living. They believe that the arguments against it can be overruled when saving the life of another person as this is what Allah wants: 'Whosoever saves the life of one person it would be as if he saved the life of all mankind' (Qur'an 5:32). This view is becoming more common.

What do the Islamic authorities say?

In 1995 the Muslim Law (Shari'ah) Council UK issued a directive (fatwa or religious opinion) supporting organ donation and transplantation stating that:

- The Council supports organ transplantation as a means of alleviating pain or saving life on the basis of the rules of Shari'ah law.
- Muslims may carry donor cards.
- In the absence of a card or an expressed wish to donate their organs, the next of kin of a dead person may give permission to donate organs to save other people's lives.

The UK Transplant Service nevertheless suggests that an individual should take the advice of their local imam or scholar if in doubt.

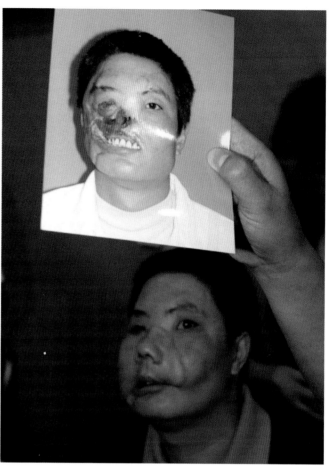

In 2006, this man had a face transplant, two years after suffering a bear attack. The photographs were taken before and after surgery.

Activities

1   Explain in your own words how Muslim beliefs about life after death affect attitudes to organ donation.

2   Now that you have learned about transplant surgery and the attitudes of Christians and Muslims towards it, what do you think? Create a short presentation which explains your own views and includes reasons why some people might disagree with you.

For discussion

Is there anything about face transplants which concerns you more than transplantation of internal organs? Is this going too far? What do you think Christians and Muslims would think about this?

Summary

- Some Muslims disagree with transplant surgery because of the teaching that the body should not be violated after death.
- The Muslim Law (Shari'ah) Council, however, has ruled that it is permissible to carry donor cards and to receive organ transplants, on the grounds that the principle of saving life must take precedence.

Know Zone
Environmental and medical issues

Quick quiz

1 Identify two sources of pollution.

2 What is the greenhouse effect?

3 Name two non-renewable natural resources.

4 Name two renewable natural resources.

5 What is IVF?

6 What is surrogacy?

7 Name one problem of fertility treatment.

8 How can a UK citizen show that they would like to donate their organs after death?

9 Which organ is the most commonly transplanted?

10 Is it legal in the UK to pay for a privately donated organ?

Find out more

For more information on the following, go to www.heinemann.co.uk/hotlinks (express code 4233P) and click on the appropriate link.

- **Wildlife trusts:** find out about local organisations that promote conservation and preservation of the environment.

- **British Trust for Conservation Volunteers:** this is a volunteer organisation that works in the local community on conservation projects.

- **Infertility support:** a website that gives help and advice regarding infertility.

- **Organ donation:** find out more about organ donation in the UK.

Plenary activity

As a group, or in pairs, create three scenarios in which a couple are infertile. Which issues should be taken into account when seeking infertility treatment? For example, a couple in their late 30s who are financially stable, and have not conceived for ten years. They already have two children in their early teens.

Take as many factors into account as you can think of, for example, religious background, age, financial circumstances. You may include an example of a same-sex couple if you wish.

Student tips

I really enjoyed studying this section as it is varied and all the issues relate to everyday life and concern many people. I became so interested in environmental issues that I volunteered to be part of a local nature reserve conservation team. If I hadn't studied this section in RS I wouldn't have even known about that kind of thing.

Self-evaluation checklist

Read through the following list and evaluate how well you know and understand each of the topics.
How well have you understood the topics in this section? In the first column of the table below use the following code to rate your understanding:

Green – I understand this fully
Orange – I am confident I can answer most questions on this
Red – I need to do a lot more work on this topic.

In the second and third columns you need to think about:

● Whether you have an opinion on this topic and could give reasons for that opinion if asked

● Whether you can give the opinion of someone who disagrees with you and give reasons for this alternative opinion.

Content covered	My understanding is red/orange/ green	Can I give my opinion?	Can I give an alternative opinion?
● The causes of global warming and possible solutions to it.			
● Forms of pollution and their possible solutions.			
● The scarcity of natural resources and how this threatens the future of the planet, with possible solutions.			
● Christian teachings on stewardship and how they affect Christian attitudes to the environment.			
● Islamic teachings on stewardship and how they affect Muslim attitudes to the environment.			
● The nature and importance of medical treatments for infertility.			
● Different attitudes to infertility treatments among Christians and the reasons for them.			
● Attitudes to infertility treatments in Islam and the reasons for them.			
● The nature and importance of transplant surgery.			
● Different attitudes to transplant surgery in Christianity and the reasons for them.			
● Different attitudes to transplant surgery in Islam and the reasons for them.			
● Your own opinion on these issues as well as why others may feel differently.			

exam zone

Know Zone
Environmental and medical issues

Introduction

In the exam you will see a choice of two questions on this section. Each question will include four tasks, which test your knowledge, understanding and evaluation of the material covered. A 2-mark question will ask you todefine a term; a 4-mark question will ask your opinion on a point of view; an 8-mark question will ask you to explain a particular belief or idea; a 6-mark question will ask for your opinion on a point of view and ask you to consider an alternative point of view.

Mini exam paper

(a) What is **surrogacy**?
(2 marks)

Just give a short, accurate definition.

(b) Do you think it is important to recycle?
Give **two** reasons for your point of view. (4 marks)

You must give two clear and properly thought out reasons – ones which you have learned in class. Always use proper English and avoid slang words like 'useless'. Think your answer through carefully first.

The word explain means you should be clear why some Muslims do not agree with transplant surgery while some do. Don't just list problems or arguments, but explain why they are problems or arguments. This question is worth 8 marks so spend a longer time on it. You will also be assessed on your use of language in this question.

(c) Choose **one** religion *other than Christianity* and explain why some of its followers agree with transplant surgery and some do not. (8 marks)

(d) 'Religion is the best way to protect the environment.'
In your answer you should refer to at least one religion.

(i) Do you agree? Give reasons for your opinion. (3 marks)

Don't make things up – use reasons you have learned in class. Don't forget to refer to a religion.

Now you must to give the opposite point of view. As before, give reasons you have learned in class. You must show you understand why people have these other views, even if you don't agree with them.

(ii) Give reasons why some people may disagree with you. (3 marks)

Mark scheme

(a) You will earn 2 marks for a correct answer, and 1 mark for a partially correct answer.

(b) To earn up to the full 4 marks you need to give two reasons and to develop them. Two brief reasons will earn 2 marks. One simple reason will only get 1 mark.

(c) You can earn 7–8 marks by giving up to four reasons, but the fewer reasons you give, the more you must develop them. You are being assessed on your use of language so you also need to take

care to express your understanding in a clear style of English, and make some use of specialist vocabulary.

(d) To go beyond 3 marks for the whole of this question, you must refer to one religion. The more you are able to develop your answers the fewer reasons you will need to give. Three simple reasons can earn you the same mark as one fully developed reason.

ResultsPlus
Maximise your marks

(b) Do you think it is important to recycle?
Give **two** reasons for your point of view. (4 marks)

Student answer	Examiner comments	Improved student answer
I think it is important to recycle because there is too much waste in the world. Recycling means that glass and paper, etc. can be made into new products.	This answer would receive 2 marks because it gives one reason and then develops it. To gain full marks, the candidate needs to add another developed reason.	I think it is important to recycle because there is too much waste in the world. Recycling means that glass and paper, etc. can be made into new products. Recycling also helps to conserve natural resources such as metals. If we don't recycle things like drinks cans, at some point we will run out of tin to make them.

Peace and conflict

Introduction

In this section you will learn about the beliefs that Christians and Muslims have about peace and conflict. You will explore the reasons why wars occur and the attitudes that Christians and Muslims have to fighting wars, as well as the work of religious organisations which work for peace. Conflict is not only international, so you will learn about the ways in which Christians, Muslims and non-religious believers address the issue of bullying and conflicts within families. Religious teaching always aims to seek reconciliation where there has been conflict, so you will also learn about how both Christians and Muslims work to ensure that conflicts are resolved.

Learning outcomes for this section

By the end of this section you should be able to:

- give definitions of the key terms and use them in answers to GCSE questions
- give reasons why wars occur, giving examples from current conflicts
- describe how the United Nations works for world peace, and give an example of their work
- explain how religious organisations try to promote world peace
- outline the nature and importance of the just war theory
- explain differences between Christians in their attitudes to war
- outline Muslim attitudes to war
- outline Christian, Muslim and non-religious attitudes to how religious conflicts occur within families and how they might be resolved
- outline Christian and Muslim attitudes to bullying
- explain Christian and Muslim teachings on forgiveness and reconciliation
- express your own opinions on the issues covered in this section and understand why some people hold views that are different from your own.

edexcel ::: key terms

aggression	exploitation	pacifism	The United Nations
bullying	forgiveness	reconciliation	weapons of mass destruction
conflict resolution	just war	respect	world peace

Fascinating fact

There have been over 250 major wars in the world since the Second World War, in which 23 million people have been killed. Three times more people have been killed in wars in the last 90 years than in all the previous 500. There are over 35 major conflicts going on in the world today.

As a group, or in pairs, discuss what experience, if any, you have of conflict. You may include any experience which you felt as conflict, for example, in your family, among your friends, or even living in a place affected by war. Talk about how you have seen people deal with conflict at home or in the world. Were those attempts successful? If not, were there better ways to do deal with it?

Come back to your answers at the end of the section and see whether your ways of thinking about conflict have changed.

An anti-war protest march in London.

For discussion

Do you think protests such as this anti-war march do any good? Why, or why not?

3.1 Why do wars occur?

Learning outcomes

By the end of this lesson, you should be able to:

- give some reasons why wars occur
- explain the reasons for the war in Darfur
- give your own opinions on why wars occur.

edexcel ⊞ key terms

Aggression – Attacking without being provoked.

Exploitation – Taking advantage of a weaker group.

The causes of war

War is an armed conflict between two or more nations. The main factors which cause nations to go to war with each other are:

Activities

1 Which of the main factors causing war do you find the most convincing and why? Which is the least convincing?

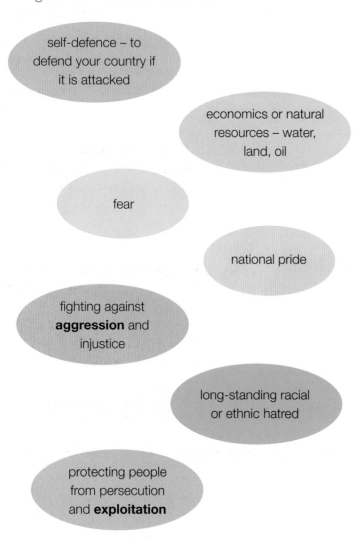

- self-defence – to defend your country if it is attacked
- economics or natural resources – water, land, oil
- fear
- national pride
- fighting against **aggression** and injustice
- long-standing racial or ethnic hatred
- protecting people from persecution and **exploitation**

However, it is important to remember that every war is unique. The reasons for war are never simple and are caused by a combination of factors.

The war in Darfur, 2003–2007 and on-going

The war in Darfur is a civil war in the west of Sudan. On one side are the Sudanese army, funded by the Sudanese government and an Arab military group called the Janjaweed. On the other side are a number of different groups, mainly non-Arab, such as the Sudan Liberation Movement and the Justice and Equality Movement.

It has been claimed by the UN that over 2.5 million people have been affected and have lost their homes and their land. The Sudanese government has been accused of mass killings and violations of human rights.

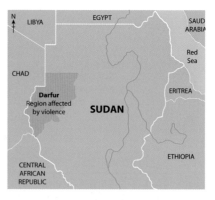

Map of Darfur showing the area affected by war.

Factor 1: economic/environment

Years of drought and increasing desertification have meant that food and water resources have become scarce. This has meant that nomadic

Activities

2 Can war ever justify suffering such as this? How would you explain the war in Darfur to these people? What do you think they would say to you?

Victims of displacement in Darfur.

people and their livestock have been forced to move south onto farmland owned by other people who are also struggling to survive. At the same time the farmers have been growing cash crops, further reducing the land available to grow food.

Factor 2: Long-standing ethnic hatred

Both sides have long-standing disputes and a traditional hatred for each other. They are divided on religious and ethnic lines. The Sudanese government has been accused of oppressing and persecuting non-Arabs and favouring Arabs.

Factor 3: National pride

The conflict in Darfur is part of a wider conflict in Sudan as a whole. Some parts of the anti-government forces (such as the Sudan Liberation Movement) want the south of Sudan to be made an independent country so they can rule themselves. The violence in Darfur was started by these forces and rapidly got worse because the government and

Activities

3 Draw an ideas map of the reasons for the conflict in Darfur. Which one of these do you think will be the hardest to overcome? Explain why.

their supporters want Sudan to stay as one country, so they fought back very aggressively.

Factor 4: Remote location

This part of the Sudan is incredibly remote with poor transport links and communications. This meant that when problems started to flare up, it took a long time for people in other countries to know what was happening and try to do something about it. By the time the international community knew what was going on, thousands had already been killed and thousands more displaced from their homes.

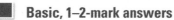

Results**Plus**

Build better answers

Choose **ONE** area of conflict in the world and explain why it is happening. (8 marks)

■ **Basic, 1–2-mark answers**
The lowest level answers give one example of conflict and provide a simple explanation for why is it happening.

● **Good, 3–6-mark answers**
Level 2 answers (3 or 4 marks) will either give a developed reason for the conflict or two simple reasons. Level 3 answers (5 or 6 marks) will either give three brief reasons, two reasons with one developed or a fully developed reason.

▲ **Excellent, 7–8-mark answers**
Most answers of the highest level will provide four brief reasons, though some will provide three reasons, one of which is developed and a few will provide two fully developed reasons. It is also possible to receive full marks for giving one exceptionally detailed reason, but it is rare for candidates to do this.

Summary

- Every war is unique but there are several factors which cause many wars, such as economic factors, ethnic hatred and self-defence.
- The war in Darfur, Sudan, was caused by many complex factors.

3.2 The United Nations and world peace

Learning outcomes

By the end of this lesson, you should be able to:

- describe and explain some of the ways in which the UN works for peace
- explain the work of the UN in Darfur
- evaluate the UN's work for world peace, and for peace in Darfur.

edexcel ⠿ key terms

Conflict resolution – Bringing a fight or struggle to a peaceful conclusion.

Reconciliation – Bringing together people who were opposed to each other.

The United Nations – An international body set up to promote world peace and co-operation.

Weapons of mass destruction – Weapons which can destroy large areas and numbers of people.

World peace – The ending of war throughout the whole world (the basic aim of the United Nations).

The United Nations

The Second World War was the most terrible war that the world has ever seen. When it was over in 1945, it was decided that an international organisation was needed to try to prevent wars to find solutions to disputes. The organisation with this role is called **the United Nations** (UN) and the process is called **conflict resolution** and **reconciliation**. There are 192 member nations, which meet regularly at the United Nations headquarters in New York.

Activities

1 Write a leaflet which explains the work the United Nations does to try to prevent and end conflict. You can find out more information about the work of the UN from their website. Go to www. heinemann.co.uk/hotlinks (express code 4233P).

UN peacekeepers in a war zone.

The United Nations is now concerned with lots of other issues as well as conflict resolution, such as fighting against poverty and campaigning for human rights. However, trying to prevent and solve conflict is still one of the UN's main aims. The UN uses a variety of methods to try to achieve peace:

- Arms control and disarmament – the UN has negotiated several treaties between countries to reduce the number and type of weapons (especially **weapons of mass destruction**).
- Organising peace talks – the UN negotiates with different parties within a conflict and communicates the issues between sides. It also arranges for leaders of the two (or more) sides to meet and discuss their issues face-to-face.
- Trade restrictions – the UN can arrange for economic sanctions to be applied, which means that certain goods decided by the UN cannot be sold to the aggressive countries. The idea is that the aggressive country must start talking and resolving the dispute so that sanctions can be lifted. In most cases, sanctions would not be imposed on things such as medicines or basic food.
- Peacekeeping forces – members of the UN can vote for soldiers from member countries to be sent to an area of conflict to try to prevent violence from breaking out or getting worse. They wear the famous 'blue helmets'. The main tasks of the peacekeepers are to protect innocent civilians and, as far as possible, to maintain food, water and medical supplies. They have to be neutral and should only use their weapons in self-defence.

- Military action – the UN also has the power to use armed force against aggressive countries. Member states have to vote for this to happen and it is very rare. An example is in 1991 when a UN force successfully drove the invading Iraqi forces out of Kuwait.

The UN has had mixed fortunes in its attempts to secure **world peace**. On the positive side, studies have found that UN peacekeepers have been successful in two out of three peacekeeping efforts and the number of wars and human rights abuses has been reduced.

It has also had its share of failures. It was unable to stop the Rwandan genocide in 1994 and Srebenica massacre in Bosnia in 1995. It was too slow to prevent the mass killings in Darfur in 2003.

A case study:
The United Nations in Darfur

We have already looked at some of the reasons for war in the Darfur region of Sudan. Now we are going to look at how the United Nations responded to this conflict.

Negotiation
It was several months after fighting broke out in March 2003 before the situation in Darfur came to light and UN requests for negotiation between the anti-government groups in the Darfur region and the Sudanese government began with little success.

There was a breakthrough in May 2004 when the Sudanese government met with the UN Secretary General. Following the talks there was a joint agreement between the United Nations and the Sudanese government to stop the conflict in Darfur. The government agreed to resume peace talks with the anti-government groups and disarm the Janjaweed. It did neither.

Since then, various peace deals have been signed and then broken between the fighting groups, but the UN have been continually successful in managing to get both sides to the negotiating table.

Threat of sanctions
Several individual countries have stopped trading with Sudan. However, as of March 2009 the UN did not have a resolution in place for economic sanctions against Sudan. This is because they have not received the number of votes required for it to happen. Several countries rely on trade with Sudan

and therefore would not vote for sanctions against them. Also, some people argue that if sanctions are put in place, the Sudanese government will stop negotiating and may prevent humanitarian aid getting through to the people who need it.

On several occasions the UN has threatened sanctions (particularly to prevent Sudan trading its oil) and this has proved effective in winning several concessions from the Sudanese government.

Peacekeeping forces
After UN negotiations (and the threat of sanctions) with the Sudanese government, a small peacekeeping force (300) from the African Union was allowed into Darfur in August 2004.

It was only in June 2007, after constant negotiation between member states of the UN (including Sudan), that it was agreed that a combined peacekeeping force from the United Nations and the African Union of 26,000 troops and police officers would to be sent into Darfur. As of March 2009, only 15,000 of these troops are in place. They have met with some success in protecting civilians, although they themselves have come under attack from both sides on several occasions.

Success or failure?
So, as of spring 2009, the United Nations has at least managed to stem the number and frequency of killings and has once again organised more peace talks between the warring parties. However, many would argue that the need for consensus among so many young people has limited the UN's ability to bring peace to Darfur so far.

Activities
2 In your own words, outline the actions of the United Nations in Darfur.

Summary
- The United Nations works for world peace in various ways.
- The UN has met with only limited success in bringing peace to Darfur.

3.3 Religious organisations and peace

Learning outcomes

By the end of this lesson, you should be able to:

- describe the work of Christian and Muslim peace organisations
- explain why religious organisations work for peace
- express your own opinions, giving reasons, as well as understand how they may differ from the opinions of others.

edexcel ⠿ key terms

Forgiveness – Stopping blaming someone and/or pardoning them for what they have done wrong.

Activities

1 Imagine you are a member of a religious minority group and the government wants to forbid your people from worshipping in that country. In pairs, discuss how you might resolve the conflict and seek reconciliation. Present your findings to the class.

Religious organisations for peace

There are a number of religious organisations who campaign in a non-violent way for world peace. They do this by:

encouraging reconciliation	educating both sides	teaching forgiveness	encouraging non-violent protest
campaigning against oppressive governments	keeping people informed of injustices around the world	encouraging opposing sides to talk to each other	speaking out against human rights abuses

Christian organisations

The World Council of Churches

The World Council of Churches (WCC) is an organisation that brings together Christians from all over the world. It works for world peace by getting those in disputes, particularly religious ones, to talk to each other and by trying to smooth things out and achieve reconciliation.

The WCC was founded in 1948 and encourages Christians of all types to work together in teaching about God and in healing the divisions between peoples of different nations and beliefs. This follows the teachings of Jesus concerning the need for **forgiveness**, peace and unity among all peoples.

The WCC supports Churches that are involved in struggles in different countries. In its 'Programme to Combat Racism', the WCC worked for peace and justice in the struggle against racism in South Africa. It has also been involved in conflicts in Sudan, Korea and Latin America.

Pax Christi

Pax Christi (Latin for 'the peace of Christ') is an international Catholic organisation set up in 1945 that works for peace all over the world. Pax Christi is opposed to war and violence and tries to get governments to solve their disputes with other nations through discussion, and economic and social justice.

'Our vision is of a world where people can live in peace and without fear of violence in all its forms. We believe in the power of prayer, reconciliation, forgiveness, justice and non-violence and the right to live in a culture which promotes these values and treats the whole of God's creation in a respectful and just manner'. (From the Pax Christi website.)

Both organisations are based on Islamic principles, because the protection of human rights and the promotion of peace and freedom are central to the teachings of Islam, '*Whoever saved a life, it would be as if he saved the life of all mankind*' (Surah 5:32).

For discussion

'Religious people should work for peace at all costs.' Do you agree?

A peace vigil organised by a Christian group.

Activities

2 Do you think a peace vigil such as the one in the photograph above does any good? Why /Why not?

3 Imagine you are an innocent victim of war. How would you respond to this photograph? Why?

Islamic organisations
Islamic Relief and the Muslim Peace Fellowship

Islamic Relief, founded in 1984, was the first Muslim agency in Europe set up to help the victims of war. It campaigns all over the world and helps those suffering as a result of war. In recent years it has worked in Bosnia, Somalia and Iraq.

The Muslim Peace Fellowship (Ansar as-Salam) works to promote world peace. It was founded in 1994 and is described as '... *a gathering of peace and justice-orientated Muslims of all backgrounds who are dedicated to making the beauty of Islam evident in the world*'. Its aims are to:

- work against injustice
- reach out to people of all faiths with a message of understanding and mutual respect
- work with everyone to bring about world peace.

A Muslim organisation promoting peace.

Activities

4 Outline the work of one Christian and one Muslim organisation to promote world peace.

Summary

- Both Christianity and Islam support organisations which work for world peace.
- Forgiveness and reconciliation are the keys to peace.

3.4 Just war theory

Learning outcomes

By the end of this lesson, you should be able to:

- define the term 'just war'
- explain the criteria needed for a war to be just
- explain the problems of the just war theory
- express your own opinions about just war, giving reasons, as well as understand how they may differ from the opinions of others.

edexcel ::: key terms

Just war – A war that is fought for the right reasons and in a right way.

Activities

1 With a partner, look up a major world conflict of the last few years on the Internet.

2 Then decide whether it fulfils the criteria of the just war theory. Present your findings to the class.

For discussion

'Religious believers should never go to war. The just war theory is nonsense.' Do you agree? Give reasons.

Activities

3 Explain the criteria for a just war in your own words, then express your own opinions about the theory – do you think that war can ever be 'just'? If so, do you agree with each of the criteria?

What is a just war?

War brings real problems for religious believers. Some consider that wars are always wrong, while others maintain that wars, though awful, may sometimes have to be fought.

To help believers with this dilemma, St Augustine suggested certain conditions which, if fulfilled, would allow a religious believer to fight in a conflict. These conditions were developed by St Thomas Aquinas and are called the **just war** theory.

These conditions cover the reasons for going to war and the conduct of the war itself. According to the just war theory, a religious believer can fight in a war if:

> There is a reasonable likelihood of success.

> It is fought with the aim to bring peace.

> It is a last resort, after all negotiations and non-violent methods of solving the dispute have failed.

> Warfare must be discriminate and civilians should not be targeted.

> The cause of war is just – such as resisting aggression and injustice.

> The methods used must be fair and reasonable.

The just war theory

Are all wars 'just wars'?

The main problem with the just war theory is that both sides in a war may claim that their cause is 'just'. For example, in the Second World War Hitler claimed that the Nazis were right and just in what they fought for, just as the allied forces did.

For discussion

Imagine you are former president George W. Bush and your partner is Osama bin Laden and you were locked in a room together. What would you ask one another and how would you reply?

Former president George W. Bush.

Osama Bin Laden, the leader of al-Qaeda.

More recently, the just war theory has been used and manipulated by skilful leaders to justify their actions and to suggest that what they have done is God's will. For example, after the invasion of Iraq, President Bush declared that the USA was the force of good, 'This will be a monumental struggle of good versus evil, but good will prevail' and defined the enemies of the USA as the 'axis of evil'.

For discussion

Does God take sides in a war?

In response, Osama bin Laden, the leader of al-Qaeda declared, 'I swear by Almighty God… that neither the United States nor he who lives in the United States will enjoy security before… all the infidel armies leave the land of Muhammad.'

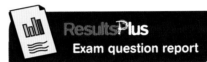
Exam question report

What is a just war? (2 marks)

How students answered

Quite a few students did not know anything about the term and offered confused answers.

Most students gave an answer that was partly correct by giving examples of just war criteria.

A few students gave a fully correct definition, such as 'a war that is fought for the right reasons and in a right way'.

Summary

- The just war theory offers conditions which enable religious believers to fight in a war.
- Some Christians believe the theory is supported by biblical teachings.
- Sometimes skilful leaders use and distort the just war theory in order to gain support for their actions.

3.5 Christian attitudes to war

Learning outcomes

By the end of this lesson, you should be able to:

● describe the teachings of the New Testament concerning war and peace

● explain the different views of Christian Churches

● express your own opinions on different Christian attitudes to war.

edexcel ⠿ key terms

Pacifism – The belief that all disputes should be settled by peaceful means.

The coalition bombing of Baghdad in the Gulf War in 2003.

Should a Christian go to war?

The Bible has a message of peace and most Christians believe that they should work towards establishing peace and ending war. Indeed, one of the titles given to Jesus was 'Prince of Peace' (Isaiah 9:6). The New Testament continually encourages Christians to seek peace, reconciliation and forgiveness. Some of the most famous of the teachings of Jesus Christ are:

'Blessed are the peacemakers, for they shall be called the children of God' (Matthew 5:9).

'Do not resist an evil person. If someone strikes you on the right cheek, turn to him the other also' (Matthew 5:39).

'Love your enemies, bless those who curse you, do good to those who hate you, and pray for those who treat you badly and persecute you' (Matthew 5:44).

'For all who draw the sword will die by the sword' (Matthew 26:52).

Activities

1 Imagine that your family had been killed in the bombing of Baghdad shown above. How do you think you would respond to the teachings of Jesus then? Would it be possible in such a situation to forgive and love your enemies? Say why, or why not.

Christians and pacifism

Pacifism means refusing to fight in wars. There are different types of pacifism:

● Absolute pacifism: no engagement in military activity at all.

● Relative or selective pacifism: no engagement in military activity in certain circumstances.

● Nuclear pacifism: no use of nuclear weapons.

A number of Christian groups, such as the Quakers, the Plymouth Brethren and Pax Christi have all refused to engage in any kind of violent struggle and have declared that they will not resist those who attack them.

> 'Quakers are (for the most part) pacifist; they do not join armies and in times of conscription are conscientious objectors. It is… a positive commitment to peacemaking and peace building.' (Quakers 'Advices and Queries')

There are four main reasons why a Christian might choose pacifism:

- The Ten Commandments forbid killing, 'You shall not commit murder' (Exodus 20:13).
- Jesus taught that people should love their enemies.
- Jesus stopped his own followers from using violence.
- Nuclear weapons and weapons of mass destruction can cause unimaginable suffering on innocent people.

Christianity and the just war theory

The just war theory is accepted now by most Christian Churches and has been used to justify many recent wars, including the World Wars, the Falklands War and the Gulf War. Christians say that there is teaching in the Bible that supports the just war theory and that, in some way, God supports such a war. The reasons why some Christians would be prepared to fight in a just war are:

- Jesus told the people they should obey the lawful government, 'Give to Caesar what is Caesar's and to God what is God's' (Mark 12:17).

- St Paul told people that Christians have a duty to obey those in authority, 'Everyone must submit himself to the governing authorities, for there is no authority except that which God has established' (Romans 13:1).

- Jesus told his disciples, '… if you don't have a sword, sell your cloak and buy one' (Luke 22:36). This means that sometimes violence may be necessary.

- Some Christians would say that there are situations where war is the lesser of two evils
- Some Christians also claim that it is right to have armed forces to protect the nation from enemies.

> 'Peace is very much at the heart of the teaching of Jesus, yet Christians have long been divided about whether it is ever right to go to war or use violence. All believe that war is wrong, but some believe that there are times when a Christian just has to go to war. This is because they believe that the result of not going to war will be much worse.' (Church of England)

Activities

2 Draw two ideas maps, one on 'why some Christians are pacifists' and the other on 'why some Christians would fight in a just war'.

3 Study your two ideas maps and decide which you most agree with. Write a paragraph under this ideas map, explaining why it is closest to your own views.

For discussion

Should a Christian follow the peace teachings of Jesus at all times? Or is it sometimes justified for a Christian to go to war?

Summary

- Christians are taught by the Bible to seek peace and reconciliation with their enemies.
- Christians have different attitudes to war, although most believe in 'selective pacifism'. Some believe in complete pacifism, while other Christians would fight in a just war.

3.6 Muslim attitudes to war

Learning outcomes

By the end of this lesson, you should be able to:

● explain the difference between the greater and lesser jihads

● explain different Muslim attitudes to war

● express your own opinions on Muslim attitudes to war.

The greater jihad

In Arabic, the word 'Islam' means 'peace'. When Muslims greet one another, they say *'salaam aleikum'*, which means 'may peace be with you'. These are both examples which show that a desire to live in peace is central to Islam. However, the Qur'an also makes it clear that this is not going to be easy.

The Qur'an teaches that, in order to follow the will of God, people will face many struggles, both inside themselves and in the world. The word for such a struggle is 'jihad'. There are two types of jihad. The first is the greater, or inner, jihad which is the struggle which Muslims should face within themselves in order to make themselves better Muslims. This involves:

● fighting against desires such as greed and envy
● doing good deeds
● visiting the mosque regularly and studying the Qur'an
● helping the poor and needy
● being a good friend and neighbour.

This greater jihad brings a believer closer to God.

Activities

1 Why is this photograph of Muslim pilgrims a good example of the greater jihad?

The lesser jihad

Although the Qur'an teaches peace, there are certain circumstances where the use of violence is permitted and there are strict rules about how wars should be fought:

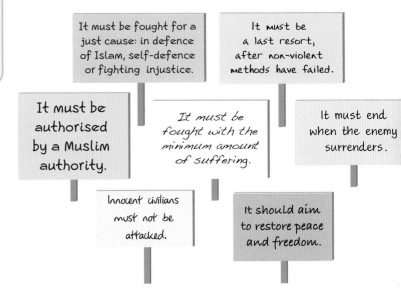

It must be fought for a just cause: in defence of Islam, self-defence or fighting injustice.

It must be a last resort, after non-violent methods have failed.

It must be authorised by a Muslim authority.

It must be fought with the minimum amount of suffering.

It must end when the enemy surrenders.

Innocent civilians must not be attacked.

It should aim to restore peace and freedom.

This is known as the lesser jihad, which means physical struggle, or war:

'Fight in the case of God those who fight you, but do not transgress the limits; for God loves not the transgressors' (Surah 2:190).

Thousands of Muslim believers at the Ka'bah, the central shrine of Islam in Mecca. They have made a long pilgrimage to get here in order to be closer to God.

For discussion

Which is the more difficult to achieve, the greater or the lesser jihad? Why?

Therefore, most Muslims believe that, under these rules, they should fight because:

- the Qur'an teaches that Muslims must fight if they are attacked
- Muhammad himself fought in wars
- many of the statements of Muhammad (hadith) permit Muslims to fight in just wars
- the Qur'an teaches that anyone who dies in a just war will go straight to Heaven.

Palestinian mourners carry the body of a child during the funeral in Gaza, where the Israelis and Palestinians have clashed for decades. Do weapons such as bombs mean that Muslim rules against harming innocent people will always be broken in modern warfare?

Muslim views against war

A growing number of Muslims believe that war or armed force is never the right response. They believe this because:

- Peace and reconciliation is at the heart of Islam and the teachings of the Qur'an.
- Modern weapons (especially nuclear weapons) cannot possibly be used in a way that is compatible with the Muslim rules about fighting in a war – innocent civilians will always be injured and killed.
- Non-violent methods are the only way to achieve peace in the end – there are always different ways to try and people should persevere.
- Violence only leads to more violence even if the 'enemy surrenders'. War only increases hatred and distrust between both sides and therefore never leads to lasting peace.

There are Muslim organisations that are founded on these principles and that try to help find peaceful solutions to conflict and speak out against war. One of these is the Muslim Peace Fellowship whose motto is: *'Whatever act of violence has just taken place, we deplore it.'*

Activities

4 Explain Muslim attitudes to war in your own words. Make sure that you include different views in your answer.

Activities

2 Compare the rules under which Muslims can fight a war with those of the just war theory in Christianity. In what ways are they (a) similar and (b) different?

3 There is a lot of misunderstanding, particularly in the West about jihad. Write a pamphlet or a presentation that explains to a non-Muslim audience what the word 'jihad' means and the difference between the greater and lesser jihad.

Summary

- Islam is concerned with the believer's struggle to find God and be a better Muslim.
- The greater and lesser jihads are paths to finding God.
- Some Muslims believe that war is never the right response.

3.7 Christian attitudes to bullying

Learning outcomes

By the end of this lesson you should be able to:

● explain what is meant by 'bullying' and some of the different types of bullying

● outline Christian attitudes to bullying

● express your own responses to bullying and Christian attitudes to it.

edexcel ▦ key terms

Bullying – Intimidating/frightening people weaker than yourself.

Respect – Treating a person or their feelings with consideration.

For discussion

Why do you think most bullying happens at school?

Should punishments for bullying in school be tougher? Why, or why not?

What is bullying?

Not all conflict is between nations. People can come into conflict as individuals and one of the most common types of personal conflict is **bullying**.

● A bully is someone who frightens others who may be weaker than themselves.

● Bullies may bully on their own or as part of a group.

● Bullies are usually older and stronger than those they bully.

● Most bullying happens in school.

● Adults may also be bullied at work by people who have more authority than they do.

Members of the 'Guardian Angels Alliance' do not carry weapons but patrol known trouble spots in the USA. They are prepared to intervene when they see bullying or aggressive behaviour against innocent people. They are not allowed to operate in the UK.

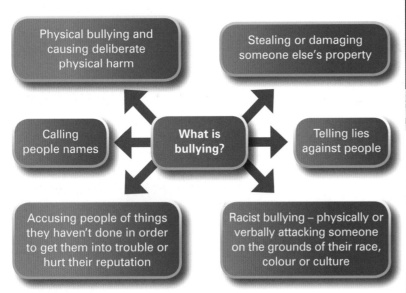

There are many reasons why people might start bullying. Bullies may:

● have problems in their family and home life

● have been victims of bullying themselves

● want to look tough

● dislike themselves, and take this out on their victims.

Activities

1 Do you think an organisation such as the 'Guardian Angels Alliance' is a good idea?

2 Why do you think they are not allowed to operate in the UK?

72

How bullying affects people's lives

The law protects people who are victims of physical and verbal bullying. Both are seen as crimes and can carry prison sentences.

Some of the possible effects of bullying.

Christians and bullying

There are no differences of opinion about bullying in Christianity – all Christians believe that it is wrong because:

- All bullying involves physical or verbal violence without a just cause, which is against all Christian teaching.
- Christians believe that every individual has been created by God and in the image of God. Therefore, bullying them would be mistreating God's creation.
- Jesus taught that people should love one another and treat other people as they would like to be treated: '...*do to others what you would have them do to you...*' (Matthew 7:12).
- Christians believe that they should treat everyone with **respect** and protect weak and vulnerable people, as Jesus taught them to do.
- Both Old and New Testaments teach that taking revenge, even against cruel behaviour, should not be done by people but by God himself.
- All Christians believe that after death they will be judged by God on the way they have lived their lives and if they have been bullies, God will not be pleased.

Anti-bullying: go to www.heinemann.co.uk/hotlinks (express code 4233P) and click on the appropriate link to find out more about Christian attitudes to bullying.

For discussion

Should the police do more to prevent bullying? How?

This Christian website advises that students being bullied at school should:

- Tell a parent or a teacher. This may be scary, especially when bullies may have threatened to do something if their victim tells a teacher. Walking Wounded suggest that it can't be worse than being bullied already.
- Pray to God for encouragement and protection and particularly to overcome feelings of fear.
- Know that God will never abandon the person being bullied, even if other people have done so in the past.

The Samaritans

The Samaritans are a well-known charity in the UK which offers telephone support to people suffering from bullying. Many Christians work as volunteers for the Samaritans.

Activities

3 Design a poster or flyer explaining Christian attitudes to bullying.

4 Describe and explain some of the ways in which Christians may help people who are bullied.

Summary

- Bullying can be physical or verbal.
- Christians are opposed to all bullying on the grounds that God's love for every individual shows it to be wrong.

3.8 Muslim attitudes to bullying

Learning outcomes

By the end of this lesson, you should be able to:

● outline Muslim attitudes to bullying

● express your own opinions about Muslim attitudes to bullying

● describe some of the ways that those being bullied can get help.

Cyber bullying is using the Internet or mobile phone technology to harass and bully people.

Islam and bullying

Like Christians, Muslims are opposed to all bullying, for whatever reason. The Qu'ran teaches *'Let there arise out of you a band of people inviting to all that is good, enjoying what is right, and forbidding what is wrong'* (Surah 3:104). This makes it clear that all Muslims should work together to challenge any wrongdoing and anything that causes harm. This includes bullying because:

● Islam teaches that any type of violence or aggression without just cause is wrong.

● Muslims believe that every individual has been created by Allah and it is wrong to abuse God's creation.

● Islam teaches that Muslims should work to put an end to injustice and cruelty, which includes bullying.

● Muhammad taught that people should protect and help the weak and the vulnerable, not attack them.

● All Muslims believe that on the Last Day they will be judged by God on the way they have lived their lives and if they have been bullies God will not be pleased.

Activities

1 Outline the reasons why Muslims disagree with all types of bullying.

2 Compare these with Christian reasons. In what ways are they similar? Are there any differences?

3 What do you think is meant by 'Islamophobia'? Explain why this has increased bullying against Muslim students in schools.

Since 11 September 2001, when terrorists who claimed to be Muslims flew planes into the twin towers in New York and killed thousands of people, there has been a big rise in the bullying of Muslim students in UK schools along with 'Islamophobia' generally. Therefore, many Muslim parents and organisations have tried to encourage schools to tackle the problem of bullying and support organisations which help the victims of bullying.

For discussion

Are physical and mental bullying equally bad?

Seeking help
Childline

'Childline aims to influence public policy and to change attitudes and practices that affect children's safety and welfare' (Childline website).

Childline is a free, confidential, 24-hour helpline for children and young people, which offers the help and support of trained counsellors to help resolve a whole range of problems. In 2003, Childline received 31,000 calls from children and, since it started, has given counselling to over one million people.

Childline has issued a number of guidelines to schools that it believes will help to solve the problem of bullying:

- Get everyone in the school to help to solve the problem of bullying – children, teachers, playground assistants, dinner staff and others.
- Put anti-bullying posters around the school and books in the library.
- Use school assemblies to explain about the problems of bullying.
- Make sure that there are plenty of staff around at break and lunchtime, when most bullying happens.
- Set up peer counselling schemes – these are groups of older pupils who give advice to younger ones. It is felt that children are better able to explain the problems of bullying than teachers are.

For discussion

Should more be done to help the victims of bullying? What measures would you like to see put in place?

Kidscape

Kidscape was founded in 1984 by Dr Michele Elliot and its aim is to teach children about personal safety and how to deal with bullying and other difficult situations. More than two million British school children have been involved in Kidscape's Child Protection Programme and 16,000 have been helped through the anti-bullying helpline.

Kidscape is an organisation that campaigns for children's safety.

In 2000, the Charity Times gave Kidscape their Charity of the Year Award.

Activities

4 Imagine your friend has been the victim of bullying in school. What would you advise them to do and why?

5 In pairs or small groups, make a poster, leaflet or presentation about bullying. You must include:
   - A definition of what bullying is, including the different types of bullying.
   - The reasons why bullying is wrong – include attitudes of Christians and Muslims as well as your own views.
   - What victims of bullying can do to try to stop it.
   - What other people and organisations can do to try to stop it.

Summary

- Muslims are opposed to all forms of bullying.
- Organisations such as Childline and Kidscape offer support to victims of bullying.

3.9 Religious conflicts within families

Learning outcomes

By the end of this lesson, you should be able to:

- give examples of situations which may cause religious conflict within families
- explain why this conflict can occur
- give some solutions to how these conflicts can be resolved
- express your own opinions on religious conflicts within families.

The causes of family conflict

Perhaps the most common area of conflict in people's everyday lives are the conflicts they experience either within their families or with their friends. There are many reasons for such conflict, for example:

Lack of progress at school

Parents splitting up or getting divorced

People trying to push their friends into doing something they don't want to do, e.g. smoking or drugs

Arguments between parents and children over their choice of friends

Problems over money

Rivalry between brothers and sisters

Conflict over moral issues – such as abortion, or parents disapproving of their child having a boyfriend or girlfriend

Activities

1 Think about conflicts within your own family. What causes the most conflict? Why do you think this is?

Religious conflicts within families

Religion and religious issues can cause conflict within a family, whether that family is religious or not. It is perhaps inevitable that many young people begin to question the beliefs and practices of their parents which they accepted as children. This can lead to conflicts about religion itself.

- A child who has had a religious upbringing may convert to a different religious faith, which would worry and concern their parents and other family members.
- A child of atheist parents may become religious, which their parents may find very difficult to understand, especially since it is likely to involve a lifestyle change.

Different generations often have different ideas about how people should live their lives anyway, and when these are combined with different religious views (or religious and non-religious views), it can cause extreme conflicts within families. Different members of the family may have different views on:

- Social behaviour – things like drinking alcohol or socialising with members of the opposite sex may cause conflict.
- Moral issues – these may cause conflict if the teachings and beliefs of a religion contradict the beliefs of another member of the family – for example, cohabiting instead of/or before marrying or choosing to have an abortion.
- Jobs and careers – the choice of job may cause conflict with the rest of the family. For example, pacifist Christian parents would not be happy if their child chose to become a soldier.

- Choice of boyfriend or girlfriend – if the child's (or parent's) boyfriend or girlfriend is from another faith, this could cause conflict.
- Raising children – grandparents often have different ideas on how to raise children from the parents and this may be heightened by religious beliefs if the grandparents have different views from the parents. For example, things like attending Sunday school or Madrassah, or sending the children to a religious school may cause conflict.

Activities

2 Draw an ideas map of all the different religious conflicts within families that you can think of. Pick two of your ideas and write a short paragraph explaining how each one may lead to conflict.

How religious families deal with conflict

Religion teaches that the relationships between family members should be based on mutual love, respect and responsibility. Christianity teaches that children should honour their father and mother (Exodus 20:12), but parents too are called not to *'provoke your children to anger'* (Ephesians 6:4).

A child taking 'time out' as a form of punishment.

Islam teaches that no child should cause harm to their parent and neither should parents cause any harm to their child. Muslims are called to obey their parents even in adulthood, and to accept the authority their wisdom and experience grants them.

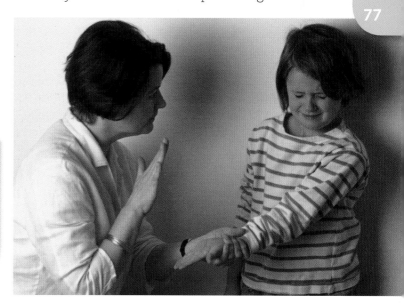

A parent punishes their child with a smack.

Activities

3 Do you think either of the punishments in the photographs would be the right thing to do?

For discussion

How can religion help to solve family conflicts?

Summary

- Conflicts within families are inevitable and may happen for many reasons.
- Christianity and Islam offer teachings on how to deal with family conflict and aim to resolve it and find reconciliation within the family.
- Some conflicts in families arise over disagreements about religious belief and practice.

3.10 Christian teachings on forgiveness and reconciliation

Learning outcomes

By the end of this lesson, you should be able to:

- define the terms 'forgiveness' and 'reconciliation'
- explain Christian teachings on forgiveness and reconciliation
- give your own opinions on Christian teachings about forgiveness and reconciliation.

What is forgiveness and reconciliation?

Christianity teaches that the way to resolve conflict is through forgiveness and reconciliation. Forgiveness means stopping blaming someone and/or pardoning them for what they have done wrong. Reconciliation means bringing together people who were opposed to each other.

The Bible teaches that people should forgive those they have had an argument or fight with, and that reconciliation is the best way to solve problems between family and friends. Christians should forgive and seek reconciliation because the Bible says:

> 'Love your enemies, do good to those who hate you.' (Luke 6:27)

> '… if you hold anything against anyone, forgive him, so that your Father in heaven may forgive you your sins.' (Mark 11:25, 26)

> '"Lord, how many times shall I forgive my brother when he sins against me? Up to seven times?" Jesus answered, "I tell you, not seven times, but seventy-seven times."' (Matthew 18:21–22)

> 'If anyone has caused you grief… you ought to forgive and comfort him.' (2 Corinthians 2:5–7)

> 'Forgive us our sins, for we also forgive everyone who sins against us.' (Luke 11:4)

One Christian family who live by this teaching are the Walkers. Their 18-year-old son, Anthony, was murdered by two men in a racially motivated attack in July 2005. The murderers were sent to prison and after the trial, Anthony's mother said, 'I've got to forgive them. My family and I still stand by what we believe – forgiveness.'

The Walker family after the murder of their son.

ResultsPlus
Watch out!

Many students struggle to know the difference between forgiveness and reconciliation – make sure you know the meanings of these key terms.

Activities

1 The Walker family offered forgiveness to their son's killers. What do you feel about their response?

2 How do you think the murderers feel?

3 Can you remember a situation in your life when someone forgave you? What happened and how did you feel?

4 Have you ever forgiven someone and been reconciled with them? What happened?

Millions of people were killed in the Holocaust in the Second World War.

The example of Jesus

Christians believe in the importance of forgiveness because God has forgiven them. Jesus died on the cross to bring forgiveness and reconciliation between God and humanity,

'For God so loved the world that he gave His one and only Son, that whoever believes in him shall not perish but have eternal life' (John 3:16). Even as he was dying, Jesus forgave his enemies, *'Father, forgive them, for they do not know what they are doing'* (Luke 23:34).

Therefore Christians should forgive others and believe that God will help them to do this even when it's difficult.

Are some things unforgivable?

Many Christians believe that, with the love of God, everything is forgivable, *'Forgiveness is the fundamental condition of the reconciliation of the children of God with their Father and of men with one another'* (Catechism of the Catholic Church).

However, other Christians would argue that if the conflict was about a religious or moral issue upon which the Bible had a definite teaching, and the person they are in conflict with is going against Christian beliefs, then there can be no reconciliation. Christian beliefs should not, therefore, be given up.

Activities

5 Explain Christian teachings on forgiveness and reconciliation.

6 **Role-play.** It is the present day and you are an elderly survivor of the Holocaust and your partner is an old soldier who was involved in the killing all those years ago. You meet by chance. What would you say to one another? How would you explain what happened? Would there be forgiveness and reconciliation between you?

Summary

• Christianity stresses the importance of forgiveness and reconciliation.

• Christians should follow the example of Jesus and forgive their enemies.

• Some believe that certain actions may be unforgivable.

3.11 Muslim teachings on forgiveness and reconciliation

Learning outcomes

By the end of this lesson, you should be able to:

● explain Islamic teachings on forgiveness and reconciliation

● give your own opinions on Muslim teachings about forgiveness and reconciliation.

Muslims, and forgiveness and reconciliation

Islam teaches that conflicts should be resolved by forgiveness and reconciliation. The meanings of these are the same for Muslims as they are for Christians – forgiveness means stopping blaming someone and/or pardoning them for what they have done wrong and reconciliation means bringing together people who were opposed to each other.

Muslims believe this because:

● One of the names of God is 'Allah, the Compassionate and Merciful'. Muslims believe that Allah forgives people and therefore Muslims should forgive people too.
● They believe that on the Day of Judgement, God will show mercy and forgiveness to those who themselves have shown mercy and forgiveness to their fellow humans.
● They believe they should follow the example and teachings of the Prophet Muhammad who taught that people should forgive and be reconciled with those who have offended them.
● There are many teachings in the Qur'an about forgiveness and reconciliation.

For discussion

Do you believe that God really can and does forgive? Why, or why not?

Some of the teachings are:

'If a person forgives and makes reconciliation, his reward is due from God.' (Surah 42:40)

'Give justice to the person who was unfair and unjust to you.' (Hadith)

'A kind word with forgiveness is better than charity followed by injury.' (Surah 2:263)

'Don't feel envy against the other.' (Hadith)

'Live as fellow brothers and sisters, as Allah has commanded you.' (Hadith)

ResultsPlus
Build better answers

Choose **one** religion other than Christianity and outline its teachings on forgiveness and reconciliation. (8 marks) June 2007

 Basic, 1–2-mark answers
These answers tend to focus on either forgiveness or reconciliation and give one simple teaching from the religion of the candidate's choice, but which is not explained in depth.

 Good, 3–6-mark answers
These answers either offer a couple of different teachings from the religion of the candidate's choice (more for 5–6 marks) with a brief explanation, or will focus on one teaching (or two for 5–6 marks) with a detailed explanation.

 Excellent, 7–8 mark answers
These answers will explain in detail at least two teachings on forgiveness and reconciliation from the religion of the candidate's choice.

Forgiveness and hajj

One very important way in which Muslims follow this teaching is during the pilgrimage (hajj), where thousands of Muslims climb Jebel al-Rahma (Mount Mercy) on the Plain of Arafat, near Mecca. They wear a simple garment called an Ihram to show equality and selflessness. They believe that, by praying on this holy spot, that God will forgive their sins.

Islam, '*On that day, the wrongdoer will bite at his hands and say: "O that I had taken the straight path! Woe is me! Would that I had never taken such a one for a friend. He led me astray."*' (Surah 25:27–30)

In September 2005, a Danish newspaper published cartoon drawings of the prophet Muhammad. Many Muslims found this to be deeply offensive to Islam and, as a result, unforgivable. Protests happened around the world and more than 100 people were killed and many Embassies destroyed.

Activities

1 Outline Muslim teachings on forgiveness and reconciliation.
2 Explain in your own words why hajj illustrates how important forgiveness is in Islam.

Activities

3 Do you agree or disagree with the protest?
4 Was the reaction of the protesting Muslims to the cartoons around the world in line with Islamic teaching. Say why, or why not?

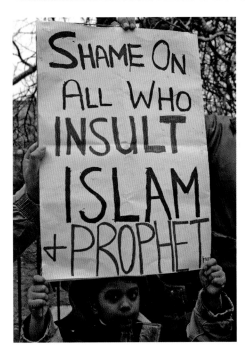

Muslims in London protesting against the Danish cartoons.

At Arafat an important part of hajj is asking Allah to forgive sins.

Are some actions unforgivable?

Some Muslims would argue that certain actions may be unforgivable, for example, working against Islam and denying Muslim principles. For this reason, Muslims are warned to avoid associating with those who may influence them away from

Summary

- Islam stresses the importance of forgiveness and reconciliation.
- Muslims should follow the example of the Prophet and forgive their enemies.
- Some believe that certain actions may be unforgivable.

examzone

Know Zone
Peace and conflict

Quick quiz

1 Give three reasons why countries may go to war.
2 Give three religious reasons why families may be in conflict.
3 Explain how bullying may affect someone's life.
4 What is forgiveness?
5 Why is forgiveness important?
6 Why do religions encourage reconciliation?
7 What is pacifism?
8 Why do some people think pacifism is wrong?
9 Was Jesus a pacifist?
10 What is jihad?

Plenary activity

As a group, create a fictional scenario of conflict. Give each other roles to play, for example, one person could be the family member or a political leader who created the conflict, someone else could be an outsider who tries to offer advice on the situation. One member of the group (or possibly your teacher) could take the role of a mediator. Discuss how each person will present their case to the mediator. After the presentations have taken place, discuss whether it would be possible for the conflict to be resolved and if so, how.

Find out more

For more information on the following, go to www.heinemann.co.uk/hotlinks (express code 4233P) and click on the appropriate link.

- **BBC History:** learn more about the world wars in the 20th century from the BBC History site.
- **CND:** find out about the long-running Campaign for Nuclear Disarmament.
- **World Peace:** the World Peace Prayer Society aims to spread peace through prayer.
- **Bullying advice:** this website offers advice about bullying for teachers, children and parents, as well as information for school projects.
- **Life challenges:** this is a Christian website that offers guidance on a whole range of problems individuals may face.

Student tips

When I studied GCSE I found it hard to be interested in issues of war because it felt so unrelated to my everyday life. However, when I understood that conflict is something which affects us all, I felt differently about it. I understood war as being like conflict in families only much bigger, but needing people to be as understanding of other's points of view. It is hard enough to do this in families, so it must be almost impossible in wartime. It made me look more critically at questions of war and I reached the conclusion that, like family conflict, war is inevitable, but it is never a good thing. I don't believe in the idea that you need conflict to grow as people. It's better to grow in a peaceful environment.

Self-evaluation checklist

Read through the following list and evaluate how well you know and understand each of the topics.
How well have you understood the topics in this section? In the first column of the table below use the following code to rate your understanding:

Green – I understand this fully

Orange – I am confident I can answer most questions on this

Red – I need to do a lot more work on this topic.

In the second and third columns you need to think about:

● Whether you have an opinion on this topic and could give reasons for that opinion if asked

● Whether you can give the opinion of someone who disagrees with you and give reasons for this alternative opinion.

Content covered	My understanding is red/orange/ green	Can I give my opinion?	Can I give an alternative opinion?
● Describe how the United Nations works for peace, including an example of their work.			
● Outline how some religious organisations try to promote world peace.			
● Explain why wars occur, using examples from current conflicts.			
● Understand the nature and importance of the just war theory.			
● Explain the different attitudes to war among Christians and the reasons for them.			
● Explain the different attitudes to war among Muslims and the reasons for them.			
● Describe Christian attitudes to bullying and the reasons for them.			
● Describe Muslim attitudes to bullying and the reasons for them.			
● Understand how and why religious conflicts within families may happen.			
● Outline Christian teachings on forgiveness and reconciliation.			
● Explain the teachings on forgiveness and reconciliation of Islam.			

exam**zone**

Know Zone
Peace and conflict

Introduction

In the exam you will see a choice of two questions on this section. Each question will include four tasks, which test your knowledge, understanding and evaluation of the material covered. A 2-mark question will ask you to define a term; a 4-mark question will ask your opinion on a point of view; an 8-mark question will ask you to explain a particular belief or idea; a 6-mark question will ask for your opinion on a point of view and ask you to consider an alternative point of view.

Here you need to explain the reasons why members of a religion other than Christianity are against bullying and not simply list arguments against it or reasons why anyone might think it is wrong. This means you need to refer specifically to religious teaching not just common-sense ideas – although sometimes they do overlap! This question is worth 8 marks so you must be prepared to spend some time answering it. You will also be assessed on your use of language in this question.

Now you have to give the opposite point of view, again, using material you have learned during your studies. You must show you understand why people have these other views, even if you don't agree with them.

Mini exam paper

(a) What is a **just war**? (2 marks)

(b) Do you think wars are always bad?

Give **two** reasons for your point of view. (4 marks)

(c) Choose **one** *religion other than Christianity* and explain why its followers are against bullying. (8 marks)

(d) 'Religious people should always forgive.'

In your answer you should refer to at least one religion. (3 marks)

(i) Do you agree? Give reasons for your opinions.

(ii) Give reasons why some people may disagree with you. (3 marks)

Here you need to give a short, accurate definition. You do not need to write more than one clear sentence

You can give your opinion, but make sure you do give two clear and thought out reasons. These can be ones you have learned in class, even if they are not your own opinion. You shouldn't use terms such as 'rubbish' or 'stupid' as these don't show that you are able to think things through carefully.

Again, you can use reasons you have learned from your studies. You need to give three simple reasons or fewer developed reasons for or against.

Mark scheme

(a) You will earn 2 marks for a correct answer, and 1 mark for a partially correct answer.

(b) To earn up to the full 4 marks you need to give two reasons (as asked) and to develop them. Two brief reasons will earn 2 marks. One simple reason will only get one mark.

(c) You can earn 7–8 marks by giving up to four reasons, but the fewer reasons you give, the more you must develop them. You are being assessed on use of

language, so you also need to take care to express your understanding in a clear style of English, and make some use of specialist vocabulary.

(d) To go beyond 3 marks for the whole of this question, you must refer to one religion. The more you are able to develop your answers the fewer reasons you will need to give. Three simple reasons can earn you the same mark as one fully developed reason.

ResultsPlus
Maximise your marks

(d) 'Religious people should always forgive.'
In your answer you should refer to at least one religion.

(i) Do you agree? Give reasons for your opinion. (3 marks)
(ii) Give reasons why some people may disagree with you. (3 marks)

Student answer	Examiner comments	Improved student answer
Part (i): I agree that religious people should always forgive because God sent Jesus to die on the cross for the sins of humans, and the least we can do is forgive others. In the Lord's Prayer it says 'forgive us our sins as we have forgiven those who sin against us'.	This would gain 2 marks for giving two simple reasons – that God sent Jesus for the forgiveness of the world, and that receiving God's forgiveness is dependent on forgiving other people.	Part (i): I agree that religious people should always forgive because God sent Jesus to die on the cross for the sins of humans, and the least we can do is forgive others. In the Lord's Prayer it says 'forgive us our sins as we have forgiven those who sin against us'. Jesus taught people to forgive their enemies every time they do something wrong.
Part (ii): Some people may disagree with me on the grounds that to forgive some people's actions is too much, if, for example, they have killed hundreds of people, or have caused terrible hurt to others. To forgive them is not to show that what they have done is wrong.	This would also gain 2 marks for developing one reason in detail.	Part (ii): Some people may disagree with me on the grounds that to forgive some people's actions is too much, if, for example, they have killed hundreds of people, or have caused terrible hurt to others. To forgive them is not to show that what they have done is wrong. Also if they are going against God's teachings some people believe they should not be forgiven.

Crime and punishment

Introduction

This topic covers issues of crime and punishment in modern society in relation to religion. You will learn what Christians and Muslims believe about the role of the law and the need for justice and punishment, including the controversial issue of capital punishment. You will then move on to look at an issue of particular concern to young people in today's society: the laws concerning the use of alcohol and drugs, and how both Christianity and Islam stand on these matters.

Learning outcomes for this section

By the end of this section you should be able to:

- give definitions of the key terms and use them in answers to GCSE questions
- explain the need for law and justice
- outline theories of punishment and the arguments for and against them
- explain why justice is important to Christians and Muslims
- describe the nature of capital punishment and non-religious arguments about it
- explain Christian and Muslim attitudes to capital punishment
- outline drug and alcohol laws and social and health problems arising from drugs and alcohol
- explain Christian and Muslim attitudes to drugs and alcohol
- express your own opinions on the issues covered in this section and understand why some people hold views that are different from your own.

edexcel ::: key terms

addiction	deterrence	law	responsibility
capital punishment	judgement	reform	retribution
crime	justice	rehabilitation	sin

Fascinating fact

Surveys and opinion polls, as well as the popular news media, suggest that more than 65 per cent, and sometimes as much as 90 per cent of the UK population would like to see the return of capital punishment, particularly in the case of serial murderers or child killers.

Starter activity

Take a sheet of A3 paper and, as a group or in pairs, identify as many issues as you can which you think are matters for the law. Then, try to organise them into their relative importance. For example, do you think murder is the most serious crime which should be punished? Do you think laws regarding alcohol are among the least important? At the end of the topic, come back to your list and see if any of your views have changed.

A young person vandalising a car.

For discussion

How does the photograph make you feel? Do you think vandalism is a matter for the law? Should this vandal be punished? Should religion have any contribution to make to this kind of issue?

4.1 The need for law and justice

Learning outcomes

By the end of this lesson, you should be able to:

- explain the need for law and justice
- describe how laws are made and justice is enforced
- give your own opinions on the need for law and justice.

edexcel ⠿ key terms

Crime – An act against the law.

Justice – The due allocation of reward and punishment. The maintenance of what is right.

Law – Rules made by Parliament and enforceable by the courts.

Responsibility – Being responsible for one's actions.

Sin – An act against the will of God.

The nature of law and justice

Laws are the rules that govern human relationships and society as a whole. Under the law, we take **responsibility** for the way we choose to behave. **Justice** is about enforcing the laws in a way that is fair and equal to everyone, making sure that good acts are rewarded and bad acts punished. A **crime** is an action that is against the law and liable to punishment.

We ought to protect weak people so that they don't get bullied

Everyone is entitled to live in peace

We need to be kept safe from criminals

People need to know how to behave with each other

I want to live without fear

We need to be protected against violence

Some views on why it is important to have laws.

Laws in the UK are made by Parliament and enforced through the police and the courts to enable people to live together in freedom, safety and order.

Activities

1 Is begging a crime? Imagine you are this beggar. How would you justify what you are doing?

A woman begging for money in London.

2 With a partner, explain why all societies have laws. What would happen if there weren't any laws?

Justice comes from the courts. When someone is accused of a crime, the courts must ensure that the law is applied properly and fairly. Without justice, the law could not operate with authority because people would believe it was unfair.

Justice, law and sin

There are many forms of moral wrongdoing which may, or may not be, against the law. A **sin** is an act that goes against the will of God. Some sins, such as murder, are also crimes, but other sins, such as adultery, are not against the law. In the same way, sometimes a crime is not a sin. For example, breaking the speed limit in order to get a sick person to hospital is a crime but not, necessarily, a sin.

However, there can be serious problems if a government makes a law which the people think is wrong or unjust. For example, in the early 1990s, the UK government issued a law requiring people to pay a community charge called the poll tax. Many people thought that the law was unfair and there was a great deal of protesting and rioting. Eventually, the government withdrew the law.

Activities

3 Should protests such as this riot be against the law?

Poll tax riot in 1990.

Challenge!

4 Explain why justice is important.

How are laws made in the UK?

Laws are made by Parliament through a very complex procedure.

First, the proposed law is written out in a document called a Bill, which is introduced and debated in the House of Commons. This is called the First Reading.

⬇

The Bill is again debated in Parliament. This is the Second Reading.

⬇

It is then passed to a committee, who go through it in detail.

⬇

It is then debated again. This is the Third Reading. Then a vote is taken and, if the vote is in favour of the Bill, then it is passed to the House of Lords for discussion.

⬇

The House of Lords debate and vote on the Bill.

⬇

If it is passed, it is then sent to the Queen who gives it the Royal Assent.

⬇

The Bill then becomes an Act of Parliament and is law.

ResultsPlus
Top tip!

Remember to learn the differences between 'law' and 'sin'. Candidates who score highly can define key terms well.

Summary

- Law and justice are vital to the smooth running of society.
- Parliament makes laws, and the police and law courts enforce it.

4.2 Theories of punishment

Learning outcomes

By the end of this lesson, you should be able to:

- describe some different theories of punishment
- explain the arguments for and against these theories
- give your own opinion about these theories and the reasons for them.

If laws are going to work, people who break the law have to be punished in some way. In the UK, a person is presumed to be innocent until they are proven guilty in court. For a minor offence, a person may be fined or sentenced to do community service work, while more serious offences carry a prison sentence. The most severe sentence in the UK is life imprisonment.

Activities

1 What do you think the right punishment should be for the offences in the photographs, as well as the ones listed below?

A drunken woman who has been binge drinking in a city centre.

The terrorist bombing in London on 7 July 2005. A woman covers her face with a burn mask, while being taken to safety.

(a) Shooting and killing a shopkeeper in order to steal their money.

(b) Stealing £5 from an old lady's purse.

(c) Parking your car and forgetting to put any money in the parking meter.

edexcel ::: key terms

Deterrence – The idea that punishments should be of such a nature that they will put people off (deter them from) committing crimes.

Reform – The idea that punishments should try to change criminals so that they will not commit crimes again.

Rehabilitation – To restore to normal life.

Retribution – The idea that punishments should make criminals pay for what they have done wrong.

Arguments for theories of punishment

Punishment is not just concerned with making sure that everyone obeys the law. There are several theories about the purpose or aims of punishment:

Deterrence

To deter someone means to prevent or discourage them from doing something that is against the law. The idea is that:

1 the person who is punished may be put off doing that action again

2 someone who may have thought about doing that action is put off by seeing the punishment that the other person received.

Retribution

This is the idea that when society punishes someone for wrongdoing it makes the victims of the crime feel a sense of justice and revenge; they feel that the offender 'got what they deserved' and should suffer for what they have done.

Reform

Some people think that punishment should also help to reform offenders, that is, it should help them to see what they have done wrong and ensure that they do not do it again. This normally means providing criminals with education and job training so that they can gain the skills they need to become law-abiding citizens again. This is known as **rehabilitation**.

Protection

People are frightened by violent criminals and one of the purposes of punishment is to protect the ordinary members of society from such offenders by keeping them locked in prison where they can do no harm.

In reality, many punishments combine some, or all of these different purposes.

Arguments against theories of punishment

All of these theories have arguments against them and debates about them too.

- Deterrence doesn't work. In the UK, prisons are crammed full to bursting point and nearly half of all prisoners commit crime again after they are released. If deterrence did work, this would suggest that those countries that have very severe punishments would have low levels of crime, which is not the case.
- In many cases retribution doesn't work either. Victims of crime often feel that the criminal has not been punished enough, so they do not feel a sense of justice having been done.
- Some people would argue that, in very serious crimes such as murder, retribution can never really be achieved anyway. The family of the victim will still be grieving their loss, no matter how harshly the murderer is punished for it.
- Some people argue that reform goes against the idea of punishing people, which is what they think punishment should be about. They would argue that teaching and educating criminals is not punishing them.

- Protection only works while criminals are locked away. At some point, most criminals are released back into society and many commit crime again.

Another kind of punishment that is increasingly being used in the UK is the idea of the criminal making amends for what they have done. Examples would be vandals of property being made to pay the cost of repairing the damage or repairing it themselves. Many people support this idea as it means that the criminal is punished while 'putting right their wrong'. The problem with this idea is that it only really works for non-violent crime.

Some people may argue that all these theories of punishment are wrong because they do not tackle the root causes of many crimes.

Summary

There are many different theories about punishments, all of which have arguments for and against them. The most common theories are deterrence, retribution, reform and protection.

4.3 Christians and justice

Learning outcomes

By the end of this lesson, you should be able to:

- explain why Christians should behave justly
- describe the work of Christian agencies seeking justice in the world
- give your own views on what justice means for Christians.

Christian teaching on justice

For Christians, justice is not only about the law or punishing criminals. Christians believe that they should behave justly, which means treating other people in a fair and just way. This is important because:

- God is a just God and people should behave in the same way.
- The Bible teaches that God wants people to behave justly.
- Jesus taught that everyone should be treated equally and fairly, for example by the rich helping the poor.
- Jesus taught that everyone should be treated in the way that they would like to be treated: '... do to others what you would have them do to you...' (Matthew 7:12).
- All of the Christian Churches teach that Christians should behave justly.
- On Judgement Day, God will judge their behaviour on Earth justly. If they have behaved justly, they will be rewarded and if they have behaved unjustly, they will be punished.

Christianity teaches that it is up to God to judge other people and that, because God is just, he will forgive all who are truly sorry for what they have done and who seriously want to change the way they live. Jesus said:

'Be merciful, just as your Father is merciful... Do not judge, and you will not be judged. Do not condemn, and you will not be condemned. Forgive and you will be forgiven.' (Luke 6:36–7)

edexcel key terms

Judgement – The act of judging people and their actions.

Activities

This painting is called 'God judging Adam'. It is by William Blake and was painted in 1795, during the reign of George III.

A modern painting entitled 'God's Justice' by Liz Swindle.

1 What differences do you notice between the two paintings?

2 What kind of **judgement** and justice do they show?

3 Which one is, in your opinion, the most accurate and why?

4 Draw an ideas map or write a paragraph on why justice and behaving justly are important for Christians.

Christians working for justice

Christian views of justice are perhaps best summed up by the words of Jesus himself:

> 'I needed clothes and you clothed me, I was sick and you looked after me, I was in prison and you came to visit me... I tell you the truth, whatever you did for one of the least of these brothers of mine, you did for me.'
> (Matthew 25:36, 40)

Christians try to bring justice into the world today by following Jesus' teaching. Many Christians try to ensure that the world's resources are shared more equally, for example by giving to charity, by working in areas of hardship or by campaigning for governments and other organisations to help poorer nations. Many Christians would also be concerned about areas of the world where people are oppressed and treated in an unjust way by the laws and punishments, so may choose to give to charities who work in these areas or campaign for things to change. Two Christian groups that campaign for justice are Christian Aid and CAFOD.

Christian Aid

Christian Aid works in areas of poverty around the world helping those in need and campaigning against injustice and oppression of the poor. It seeks to change the policies of governments in rich countries by campaigning for an end to the unjust debts that they have imposed upon the poorer nations.

Christian Aid supporters protesting against injustice in 2006.

CAFOD

CAFOD, or the Catholic Fund for Overseas Development, campaigns for justice for the poor of the world and in recent years has campaigned against landmines, the debt owed by the Third World, and for rich nations to take a more active role in helping the poor and oppressed. 'CAFOD's mission is to promote human development and social justice in witness to Christian faith and Gospel values' (CAFOD mission statement).

Summary

- Justice is important to Christians because they believe that God is just and wants people to behave justly and treat others equally and fairly.
- Many individual Christians and Christian agencies work for justice today.

4.4 Muslim attitudes and justice

Islamic teachings on justice

Muslims believe that God is just and, on the Last Day, will reward those people who have done good things and punish those people who have done bad things. Muslims believe in the importance of justice because:

- the Qur'an teaches that God wants people to act in justice and fairness to each other
- everyone is equal under Islamic law
- justice is the basis of Zakah (one of the pillars of Islam)
- the Shari'ah (law of God) requires justice for everyone
- the prophet Muhammad acted with justice.

Therefore, Islam teaches that Muslims should treat one another justly and should work against injustice:

> 'O ye who believe! Stand out firmly for justice, as witnesses to God...'
> (Surah 4:135).

The law of God

Muslims believe in following the law of God, which is called Shari'ah law. However, Muslims also believe that they must obey the laws of the country they are in, even if those laws are not Islamic. In the UK, some Shari'ah courts exist and are allowed to settle minor disputes between Muslims in family cases and financial matters. All Shari'ah courts have very strict rules, so that they are fair. For instance, all trials have to be public so that justice can be seen to be done and a judge should not try a case when he is angry, hungry or distracted.

A Shari'ah court in the UK.

Activities

1 Explain in your own words, why justice is important to Muslims.

2 In what ways are the teachings of Islam about justice similar to Christianity? In what ways are they different?

Activities

3 Is it a good thing to have Shari'ah courts in the UK? Give reasons for and against before making your decision.

However, Shari'ah law is not just about dealing with disputes or (in Islamic countries) crimes. It also includes rules which Muslims believe help society to operate justly with fairness to everyone. One example of this is the Shari'ah laws on making money fairly, which includes not allowing people to make money from money. This means that interest cannot be charged on loans. Most Muslims would argue that this is just, because interest makes the rich richer and the poor poorer.

For discussion

Is it a good thing to charge interest on loans or is it unjust?

Is the Day of Judgement something to fear, or to look forward to?

Muslims working for justice

All Muslims work for justice through one of the Five Pillars of Islam – Zakah. Part of this is a tax of 2.5 per cent on every Muslim's income and this is given to the poor. In this way, wealth is shared, and this helps to create a more equal and just society. As part of Zakah, Muslims are encouraged to give Sadaqah. This is either giving money to charity voluntarily or acting in a charitable way. '*Zakat creates love and brotherhood between rich and poor, it minimises social tension and bridges the gap between them and it provides social and economic security for the whole society*' (Islamic Relief Zakat Guide).

Most importantly of all, for Muslims, is the knowledge that God is watching everything that a person does and every deed is recorded in preparation for the Day of Judgement.

Two Muslim groups that campaign for justice are Muslim Aid and Islamic Relief.

Muslim Aid

Muslim Aid is an organisation that works to relieve poverty around the world and seeks to secure justice for the poor and oppressed. It has campaigned hard to persuade rich nations to be more generous in their giving to the poor and has sought to get rid of oppression in areas of great poverty and deprivation.

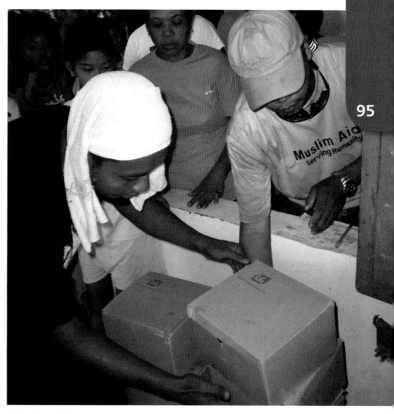

Muslim Aid at work.

Islamic Relief

Islamic Relief seeks to improve the lives of people affected by poverty, wars and natural disasters. It provides emergency food and medical relief and supports projects which provide long-term solutions to basic needs.

Activities

4 Explain how the work of Muslim charities such as those mentioned on this page are fulfilling Muslim teachings on justice.

Summary

- The Qur'an teaches that Muslims should act with justice and fairness.
- The Law of God requires fairness and justice for all.
- Many Muslims campaign for peace and justice throughout the world.

4.5 Non-religious arguments about capital punishment

Learning outcomes

By the end of this lesson, you should be able to:

- give non-religious reasons for and against capital punishment
- express your own views on the death penalty.

What is capital punishment?

Capital punishment, or execution, means taking away the life of a condemned prisoner. It is also called the death penalty.

The death penalty was abolished in the UK in 1973, except in cases of treason, and abolished completely in 1998. The last two people executed were convicted murderers, Peter Allen and John Walby, who were hanged on 13 August 1964.

Under the European Convention on Human Rights, which Britain signed in 1999, execution was abolished throughout the European Union. Other nations, including some states of the USA, still have the death penalty, although 12 states and the District of Columbia have banned it. It is estimated that there is one legal execution nearly every day, somewhere in the world, with the greatest number being in China. Methods include hanging, lethal injection, the electric chair, beheading and firing squad.

There have been many debates over the years, in the UK and elsewhere, about whether or not the death penalty is an effective punishment, and there are persuasive arguments both for and against.

A chamber where prisoners who have received the death penalty have a lethal injection.

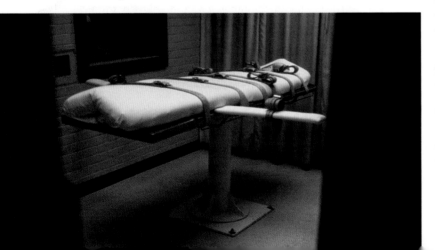

edexcel key terms

Capital punishment – The death penalty for a crime or offence.

Activities

1 Discuss how it makes you feel thinking of a prisoner being put to death.

A protester at the 3rd World Congress against the Death Penalty held in Paris in 2007.

Activities

2 Discuss whether you think the death penalty should be limited to certain people or certain crimes. For example, does it seem worse to you that a woman should be executed than a man? What about child executions, which are still carried out in some countries?

3 Should the death penalty be reserved only for murder, or do you think any other crimes may warrant it?

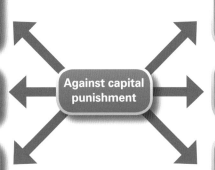

The death penalty acts as a warning and stops people committing the crime because they know they will be killed if they are caught.

The value of human life is made clear by executing those who kill others.

It can make the criminal confess to their crime as, in countries which use the death penalty, plea bargaining can reduce the sentence from execution to a life imprisonment.

For capital punishment

The death penalty means that society can rid itself of the most dangerous people, so they cannot be a threat again.

Execution is compensation for taking the life of another and may help the victim's family.

It has a good psychological effect on the population, who approve the view that bad things will happen to bad people. The Japanese, for example, execute around 3 people a year and support the death penalty on these grounds.

In those countries which have the death penalty, the number of murders does not seem to drop; the possibility of execution is no deterrent to someone considering such a major crime.

Many people have been executed who were later discovered to be innocent.

Some people believe that execution is nothing more than 'murder' by the state. This poses the question: how can a state forbid murder when it kills its own citizens?

Against capital punishment

Human life is vitally important whatever a person has done, and should not be taken away for any reason.

Terrorists who are executed can end up as heroes and this encourages further terrorism.

Some people feel that execution is an easier punishment than life imprisonment and some criminals would actually prefer it to a custodial sentence. This removes the fear factor of having the death penalty.

Activities

4 Explain four arguments for capital punishment and four arguments against capital punishment. Which do you agree with?

For discussion

Do you think that, taking all the various views into account, that the death penalty is an effective punishment or not?

Would you like to see the death penalty re-introduced into the UK? Say why, or why not.

Summary

- Capital punishment is the death penalty for a criminal offence.
- There are many strong arguments against the death penalty, including that it violates the principle of the sanctity of life and is not a true deterrent.
- Arguments in favour of it include that it is true retribution and gives the families of victims some real closure.

4.6 Christian attitudes to capital punishment

Learning outcomes

By the end of this lesson, you should be able to:

- explain why some Christians are against capital punishment
- explain why other Christians are for capital punishment for serious crimes
- evaluate these reasons and come to your own conclusions.

Against capital punishment

Christian arguments for and against the death penalty use some of the same reasoning that is found in non-religious arguments. However, they are also able to make further arguments based on their beliefs.

The crucifixion of Jesus was a Roman method of capital punishment usually used for the most dangerous criminals.

Christians who believe that the death penalty is wrong argue that:

- It goes against the sanctity of life. Only God has the right to give life and take it away.
- Jesus came to save and reform people – an executed criminal cannot be reformed.
- Jesus taught that revenge is wrong:
  'You have heard that is was said, 'Eye for eye, tooth for tooth.' But I tell you, do not resist an evil person. If someone strikes you on the right cheek, turn to him the other also.' (Matthew 5:38)
- Most Christian Churches have spoken out against capital punishment.
- Capital punishment is not compatible with the overall message of Christianity, which is one of love and forgiveness.

For discussion

Do you think that most Christians understand that Jesus was condemned as a capital offender? Should this fact make them more supportive of the death penalty or less?

For capital punishment

However, other Christians believe that the death penalty may be used for serious crimes. Their arguments may include:

- The Old Testament teaches that capital punishment should be used for some criminals: *'Whoever sheds the blood of man, by man shall his blood be shed.'* (Genesis 9:6)
- In the New Testament, St Paul teaches that Christians should accept and obey the laws and punishments of the government of the country they are living in, which would include accepting the death penalty.
- Jesus never taught that the death penalty was wrong.

- In the Middle Ages, the Christian Church itself used the death penalty against those who challenged the authority of the Church, so it cannot be wrong.
- Some Christian Churches (such as the Catholic Church) permit the death penalty for very serious crimes.

Among those Christians who agree with capital punishment, very few would agree with the death penalty for offences other than murder.

Activities

Reverend Paul Hill was put to death in 2003 for the murder of Doctor John Britton and his assistant James Barrett whom he, Hill, believed carried out abortions at a clinic in Florida. Hill knew he would be caught for the murder and that he would face the death penalty. He claimed that he felt no remorse for his crime and that he expected to receive a heavenly reward.

1   Do you think that the Reverend Paul Hill should have been executed for his crime?

2   The death penalty was not a deterrent to him. Does this suggest that the death penalty is meaningless, at least in some cases?

Activities

3   Make two lists – one of all the arguments you can think of for reasons why some Christians might agree with the death penalty and another of reasons why some Christians might disagree with it. Remember that you can use non-religious arguments as well as religious reasons if you think a Christian might use them.

ResultsPlus
Exam question report

Explain why there are different Christian attitudes to capital punishment. (8 marks) June 2007

How students answered

Many candidates scored poorly on this question because their answers were generally about capital punishment, but either did not identify Christian attitudes in any detail or they grouped all Christian attitudes together.

Most of the candidates who scored 4 marks for this question explained two different Christian attitudes with reasons. Those who scored 5 or 6 marks for this question gave two different Christian attitudes and briefly explained why there were different attitudes.

There were some excellent answers that gave a detailed response to different Christian attitudes and explained the religious teachings those believers used to justify their beliefs.

Summary

- Some Christians are strongly opposed to the death penalty because it goes against Christian teaching on the value of life, on leaving matters of judgement in God's hands, and it achieves no good purpose.
- Other Christians support it because it seems to be permitted in the Bible and has been used over the years by Christians working in conjunction with the secular authorities.

4.7 Muslim attitudes to capital punishment

Learning outcomes

By the end of this lesson, you should be able to:

● describe what the Qur'an says about capital punishment

● explain why many Muslims are in favour of the death penalty for certain crimes

● explain why some Muslims are against the death penalty

● give your own views on these ideas.

Activities

1 Search the Internet to find out the position of different Muslim countries around the world on the death penalty.

2 Which countries have carried out the most executions and which the least? Are they Muslim countries?

Shari'ah law and capital punishment

The Qur'an teaches that capital punishment may be applied for some crimes, *'Take not life – which God has made sacred – except for just cause'* (Surah 17:33). So what are these 'just causes'?

'The shedding of the blood of a Muslim is not lawful except for three reasons: a life for a life, a married person who commits adultery and one who turns aside from his religion and abandons the community.'
Hadith (quoted by Bokhari and Muslim)

Saddam Hussein was overthrown in April 2003 by a United States-led invasion and he was arrested later that year. In November 2006 Hussein was found guilty of crimes against humanity and was sentenced to death. His execution took place in December 2006. Many Muslims would agree that Saddam Hussein deserved the death penalty. Would you agree?

In all countries where Shari'ah law is the law of the land, the death penalty can be used. The crimes that carry the death penalty in Muslim countries today vary, but may include murder, rape, homosexual acts and apostasy (a Muslim denying, or working against, Islam). The number of times that it is actually used as a sentence also vary enormously in the different countries, as does the method of execution.

According to the Qur'an:

● The death penalty can only be given after a fair trial and as a last resort after the consideration of all other options.

● The victim (or the victim's family in the case of murder) has to agree to the sentence. If they do not want the criminal to be executed, then they cannot be and another sentence, such as paying compensation, will be given.

The criteria under which the death penalty can be given for some offences is very strict. For example, for someone to be condemned to death for adultery, four witnesses have to testify that they saw it taking place. During Muhammad's own lifetime, nobody was executed for adultery.

Muslims in favour of capital punishment

The reasons why many Muslims agree with the death penalty for serious crimes are:

- The Qur'an, which has come directly from Allah, says that the death penalty can be given for certain crimes.
- Shari'ah law says that the death penalty can be given for certain crimes.
- Muhammad made many statements that showed that he agreed with the death penalty.
- When Muhammad was the ruler of Medina, he himself sentenced people to death for committing murder.

Many Muslims who are in favour of capital punishment do so because of non-religious reasons (see pages 96–97) as well as religious ones. For example, Islamic philosophy teaches that punishments should be harsh because this then acts as a deterrent for other people. This is why, in some Muslim countries, executions are carried out in public.

Muslims against capital punishment

There are an increasing number of Muslims who disagree with the use of the death penalty. Some of their reasons are:

- The scholars of Shari'ah law do not agree on when or how the death penalty should be applied.
- The Qur'an says that capital punishment is an option which can be considered – it doesn't have to be used.
- The Qur'an gives such strict conditions under which the death penalty can be given (see page 100) that these are very rarely met and therefore the punishment should not be given.
- In some countries Shari'ah law is not applied properly – such as the trial not being fair – and it has also been used to oppress women and the poor who receive the most sentences of capital punishment. This goes against the teachings of the Qur'an.

Activities

3 Make two lists – one of all the arguments you can think of for reasons why some Muslims might agree with the death penalty and another of reasons why some Muslims might disagree with it. Remember that you can use non-religious arguments as well as religious reasons if you think a Muslim might use them.

ResultsPlus
Top tip!

Remember that you can never say that 'all' Muslims or 'all' Christians believe something, even if the majority of them do. There are always differences of opinion and you will only get good marks in the exam if you remember this!

Summary

- Islam is, in principle, in favour of the death penalty and the Qur'an lays out for which offences it may be given.
- There is a small, but growing, group of Muslims who are in favour of abolishing the death penalty.

4.8 Drugs and alcohol laws

Learning outcomes

By the end of this lesson, you should be able to:

● describe the basic laws regarding the sale and consumption of drugs and alcohol in the UK

● express your own opinions on these laws.

What is a drug?

Although the word 'drug' is often used to talk about illegal substances, a drug is actually any chemical that you take into your body which changes your mood or the way you feel. Most people use some sort of drugs every day, for example, by drinking tea or coffee which contains the drug caffeine. Tea, of course, is fairly harmless but there are other, more powerful drugs which are controlled by UK law in order to protect people.

• Some drugs such as alcohol and tobacco can be very damaging to a person's health.
• People can become addicted to some drugs, making it very difficult to give them up, and ruining lives.
• Children need to be protected from some drugs for as long as possible as they may cause them harm.
• Some drugs cause considerable social problems.

Different kinds of drugs

Stimulants affect the central nervous system. This increases brain activity. Stimulant drugs include cigarettes, amphetamines and cocaine.

Depressants have the opposite effect, slowing down brain activity. Alcohol and solvents (glue) are both depressants.

Hallucinogenics are drugs that change your senses and give the impression that things are there when they are not. LSD, magic mushrooms and cannabis are hallucinogens.

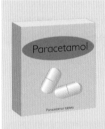

Analgesics are painkilling drugs. Aspirin® and Paracetamol® are both analgesics, as is heroin. While the former are legal and can be sold in the shops, heroin is not.

Legal and illegal drugs

Legal drugs are sold under controlled conditions in pharmacies, supermarkets and other shops.

Activities

1 Many people believe that cannabis should be available legally in the UK. Find out some arguments in favour of this move. Do you agree? Discuss your answers in pairs.

A pro-cannabis demonstration.

Children under 16 are not allowed in a pub or bar unless accompanied by an adult. Under 18s are not allowed to drink alcohol in a pub or bar. The only exception is where persons aged 16 or 17 are having a table meal in the company of someone over 18.

Alcohol can now be served up to 24 hours a day in licensed premises.

UK ALCOHOL LAWS

It is illegal for anyone under 18 years of age to buy, or try to buy, alcohol.

It is also an offence for anyone to buy, or try to buy, alcohol on behalf of a child.

Everywhere which sells alcohol has to have a licence granted by their local authority.

Some can be sold over the counter, others only on presentation of a doctor's prescription. Prescription drugs of any kind cannot be purchased by anyone under 18 years old. It is illegal to use or sell prescription drugs without a prescription.

Some non-prescription drugs are legally available in the UK (including alcohol and tobacco) but are still subject to laws regarding their sale. Other drugs such as cannabis, ecstasy and heroin are illegal. All illegal drugs are classified according to how dangerous they are. Taking or selling Class A drugs such as cocaine and heroin carries the highest penalties. Lower penalties are given for possession and supply of lower class drugs such as cannabis, but this does not mean that they are safe.

If the police have reasonable grounds to suspect that someone is in possession of an illegal drug, they can stop and search them in the street. Someone with a small amount of a drug such as cannabis may be cautioned, but penalties could be as great as imprisonment.

Activities

2   Alcohol can only be sold after 12 noon in the UK on Sundays, and in many states in the USA it cannot be sold at all on Sunday. Do you think it is right that there should be different laws for the sale of alcohol on Sunday? Do they make any difference, and, if so, to what?

Summary

- The potentially dangerous nature of drugs and alcohol means that their sale and consumption is controlled by law in the UK.
- Laws on drugs are intended to protect those consuming them and to limit the ways in which they can be sold.

4.9 Social and health problems caused by drugs and alcohol

Learning outcomes

By the end of this lesson, you should be able to:

● explain some of the social and health problems caused by drugs and alcohol

● give your own opinions on the health and social problems of drugs.

edexcel key terms

Addiction – A recurring compulsion to engage in an activity regardless of its bad effects.

Drugs and alcohol can cause some of the problems shown in the diagram:

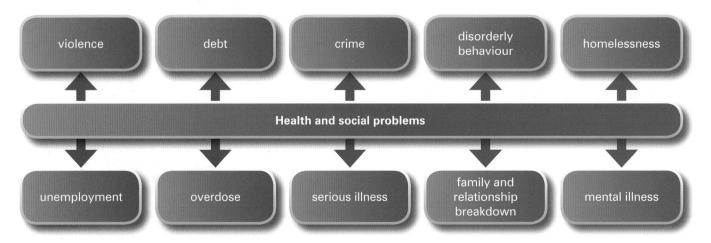

violence | debt | crime | disorderly behaviour | homelessness

Health and social problems

unemployment | overdose | serious illness | family and relationship breakdown | mental illness

Activities

1 Study the diagram and link the different consequences with different kinds of drugs: illegal substances, alcohol and tobacco. Then jot down a short explanation how or why the drugs may cause these things to happen.

Alcohol

In 2003, the Prime Minister's Strategy Unit reported that:

● Around 40 per cent of Accident and Emergency admissions are alcohol-related.

● Alcohol is associated with between 15,000 and 22,000 deaths every year.

● Up to 1.3 million children in the UK are affected by parental alcohol problems.

● Under-16s who do drink are drinking twice as much today as they did ten years ago.

● Around 50 per cent of homeless people are alcoholics.

● Almost half the victims of violent crime say their attacker was under the influence of drink; and 45 per cent of victims of domestic violence said their attacker had been drinking.

● Young white, unskilled males are likely to drink the most heavily of all people.

An average pint of lager is two units of alcohol. According to the Department of Health, men should not drink more than three to four units of alcohol a day, and women should drink no more than two to three. These guidelines apply whether someone drinks every day, once or twice a week, or occasionally. Twice the recommended amount and beyond is classed as binge drinking. Research suggests that binge drinking is on the increase among young people.

The health problems of excessive alcohol use include heart disease, stroke, liver disease and cancer. Psychological and emotional breakdown are also higher among heavy drinkers.

Smoking

Since smoking in an enclosed public space became illegal, the number of smokers has decreased. However, this is not the case among young people. Research suggests that one quarter of 15-year-olds (both boys and girls) in the UK are regular smokers and that approximately 450 children per day start smoking. If they continue to smoke throughout their lives, one half of this number will die, on average, 23 years earlier than if they didn't smoke. The biggest increase in smoking has been among teenage girls.

Activities

2 Do you think smoking should be made illegal? Discuss this question as a class and draw up a list of the advantages and disadvantages of doing so.

Smoking leads to a range of health problems, including cancer, lung disease and high blood pressure. Smokers are more likely to have poor dental health and to smell of nicotine and smoke, while the addictive habit can interfere with romantic and other social relationships.

Drugs

The negative effects of illegal drugs range from higher incidences of crime as addicts look for ways to fund their **addiction**, to unemployment and social disorder. Drug taking has a serious effect on the health of addicts who lose the incentive to work and maintain their regular lifestyle. Not only do they face the danger of a fatal overdose, but also

serious psychological effects of drug addiction even after kicking the habit. Drugs can have a serious effect on the brain, leading to mental illness and loss of brain function.

Activities

3 Discuss whether you think Amy Winehouse is a good role model for young people. On the one hand she is a talented and successful musician, on the other her life has been broken by drugs.

4 Should young people support her by buying her music?

Singer Amy Winehouse has been open about her drug problems but this does not seem to have made it easier for her to deal with them.

Summary

- The health and social problems of drugs, including smoking tobacco, and excessive drinking of alcohol are well documented.
- They range from unemployment and homelessness to heart disease, cancer and premature death.
- Drinking and smoking are both on the rise among young people and illegal drugs more easily available.

105

4.10 Christian attitudes to drugs and alcohol

Learning outcomes

By the end of this lesson, you should be able to:

● describe and explain Christian attitudes to illegal drugs

● explain different Christian attitudes to alcohol

● evaluate Christian views and compare them to your own.

Activities

1 Study the reasons why Christians believe that taking illegal drugs is wrong. Which reasons do you agree with? Explain why.

Humans as God's creation

The Bible teaches that God created our bodies and that we should not abuse them.

Although there are different Christian attitudes to alcohol, the vast majority of Christians believe that taking any kind of drug excessively damages the body that God created and is therefore wrong.

All Christians in the UK believe that taking illegal drugs is wrong because:

● the Bible teaches that Christians must obey the law of the land in which they are living, which includes the laws on drugs

● they believe that illegal drugs have been made illegal because they are the most damaging for people and Christians should not harm their bodies

● many illegal drug users turn to crime to get money to buy drugs

● drug abuse can break down marriages and family relationships, and can make people anti-social

● illegal drugs can have a powerful effect on people's behaviour and can make them behave badly or act in ways that Christians should not.

Unlike illegal drugs, alcohol and tobacco are not 'forbidden' by Christianity and therefore some Christians do smoke and/or drink. Most Christians would choose not to smoke as even a small amount of smoke can cause harm to the body.

Reasons for drinking alcohol in moderation

Many Christians do choose to drink alcohol in small amounts; this is because:

● the Bible does not forbid the drinking of alcohol

● Jesus himself drank wine and even performed a miracle that turned water into wine at a wedding.

● during the Last Supper, Jesus gave his disciples wine during the first Holy Communion or Eucharist

● St Paul told his friend Timothy to drink wine to help with digestion, so he cannot have been against drinking alcohol

● many Christian Churches, such as the Roman Catholic Church and Church of England, do not forbid the drinking of alcohol and use it during Holy Communion today.

Jesus offered wine to the disciples at the Last Supper, making it an enduring image of his death and suffering.

Teenagers smoking and drinking in a park.

For discussion

Many Christians who do not think drinking alcohol is a sin, would consider that it is better to avoid alcohol and not to start smoking. What does the photograph of teenagers smoking (above) suggest to you? Do you find it troubling or too everyday to be concerned about? Is it only Christians who would be concerned about it?

None of the teachings suggest that drinking alcohol is sinful. However, there are many teachings which warn against drinking too much because it is getting *'drunk on wine which leads to bad behaviour'* (Ephesians 5:18). Therefore, Christians who do drink alcohol do so in moderation.

Why some Christians don't drink

There are some Christians today who choose not to drink any alcohol at all. This view is associated particularly with some evangelical conservative groups and The Salvation Army. These groups believe that, although there is nothing 'sinful' about drinking alcohol, the best course of action is to avoid it because:

- drinking any alcohol can impair a person's judgement and reduce their ability to act in a Christian way

Activities

2 Some Churches do not use alcoholic wine for their communion services. What reasons might they have for doing this? Do you think that they are good reasons?

3 Draw a table of all the different Christian attitudes to alcohol. Write your own views on drinking alcohol in the final column.

- people drank wine in biblical times because there was little else for them to drink – as there are lots of other types of drink available there is no need for alcohol
- in biblical times people drank wine or ale only; today alcohol is much stronger and therefore more dangerous than it was then
- some Christians believe that drinking any alcohol is wrong so it is better not to drink it to avoid offending others.

Although, it is very rare, there are a few Christians who believe that alcohol should be made illegal such as some American Baptists. Their view is that alcohol is an evil and should be banned from society completely.

Summary

- Christians are totally against the taking of illegal drugs for all the same reasons that non-religious people are opposed to them, but also because the unbalancing of the mind caused by drugs makes it impossible to have a meaningful relationship with God.
- Christians have different attitudes to alcohol, but none would encourage drunkenness or the misuse of alcohol.

4.11 Muslim attitudes to drugs and alcohol

Learning outcomes

By the end of this lesson, you should be able to:

- describe Muslim attitudes to drugs and alcohol
- give reasons for these attitudes
- evaluate these attitudes and compare them to your own opinion.

For discussion

'Muslim attitudes to alcohol are right – look at the problems it causes in the UK.'

Muslim attitudes

All Muslims see alcohol and illegal drugs as intoxicants that should not be taken by Muslims. This is because:

- all Muslims believe that their bodies were created by Allah and should be looked after until Judgement Day; people therefore have a responsibility not to abuse their bodies with drugs and alcohol
- the Qur'an says that intoxicants are *haram* (forbidden)
- Muhammad said they should not be taken and taught about the dangers of using them (see adjacent box)
- the effects of drugs would mean that Muslims would not be able to pray or perform their religious duties properly and they would therefore interfere with their relationship with Allah
- the effects of drugs mean that Muslims would be more likely to commit other sins
- all Muslims should obey the law of the land in which they live and for British Muslims this would include the laws on illegal drugs. In many Muslim countries alcohol is illegal and processing drugs carries very severe punishments.

Some Muslims do smoke tobacco and this is seen as a personal choice, although many Muslims do not agree with smoking because of the harm that it can do to the body.

Muslim teachings

The Qur'an teaches that Muslims should avoid all intoxicants because drugs and alcohol can affect a person badly and hinder them in their daily lives, and in their relationships with other people and Allah. The Qur'an says: *'O you who believe! Intoxicants and gambling... are an abomination of Satan's handiwork: Shun such abomination, that you may prosper'* (5:93).

Muslims use stories and examples to show how drinking alcohol leads to bad decisions and to further sin. The Prophet therefore referred to alcohol as 'the mother of all sins'. The following story is used as an example.

'Once a pious man met a woman who invited him to commit a sin. The man flatly refused. After her constant insisting, she still failed. Thereafter, she gave him a choice of options: to commit adultery with her or to murder her newly born child or to consume some alcohol which she possessed. If he were not willing to comply then she would scream and falsely inform the inhabitants of that place that he had raped her. The man upon pondering decided to consume the alcohol, taking it to be least harmful of the three sins. Upon the consumption of alcohol, he became intoxicated, and then consequently, he killed the child and also committed adultery with the woman.' (Hadith 7).

Many Muslims will not sell alcohol as part of their business or work for a company that sells alcohol. Other Muslims believe that this is okay as non-Muslims will be buying the alcohol.

Activities

1 Explain in your own words why Muslims would not take illegal drugs or drink alcohol.

2 Compare Muslim attitudes to Christian ones. In what ways are they similar? How are they different? Which are closer to your own views?

For discussion

What do you think about the situation reported in *The Sunday Times*? How would you handle this as (a) an employer and (b) a Muslim employee?

Should Muslims sell alcohol to non-Muslims?

In *The Sunday Times* in September 2007 it was reported that some branches of Sainsbury's were excusing Muslim checkout staff from handling alcohol bought by customers, especially during Ramadan. Sainsbury's said they were keen to accommodate all religious beliefs, but some Muslim leaders said that the checkout staff were already going against Muslim teaching by working in a shop which sold alcohol. Others said that it made Muslims look like difficult employees and it was an overenthusiastic application of Islamic principles.

ResultsPlus
Build Better Answers

Do you think that UK laws protect people from the dangers of alcohol and drugs?
Give **two** reasons for your answer. (4 marks)

■ **Basic, 1-mark answers**
These answers tend to focus on the UK laws themselves and do not give their own opinions about how well they protect people.

● **Good, 2–3-mark answers**
These answers will give the opinion of the student along with some basic reasons which lack depth.

▲ **Excellent, 4-mark answers**
The best answers will explain their opinions in depth whether they agree or disagree with the question.

Summary

• Islam strongly forbids the use and sale of all alcohol and other intoxicants, including drugs.

• Islam teaches that use of alcohol can lead only to bad consequences and it should be considered totally *haram* in all cases.

Know Zone
Crime and Punishment

Quick quiz

1 What is the law?

2 What is justice?

3 What is rehabilitation?

4 What is retribution?

5 Name two methods of capital punishment.

6 Name two countries where capital punishment is still legal.

7 Give two arguments for capital punishment and two against.

8 Why do Muslims forbid the use of alcohol?

9 Is it legal for your parents to allow you to grow cannabis at home for your own use?

10 Did Jesus drink alcohol?

Plenary activity

As a class, organise a debate on the reintroduction of capital punishment into the UK. You will need at least one person to propose the motion that it should be reintroduced and one person to oppose it. Ask your teacher to chair the debate. Each side in the debate needs to work out a clear case for their position and the rest of the class should prepare questions they want to ask. For example, you might ask what crimes it should be applied to, or whether some methods are considered more acceptable than others.

At the end of the debate, take votes and see which side has won. Then ask yourselves whether they won because of the quality of their argument or because you already thought their views were the right ones.

Find out more

For more information on the following, go to www.heinemann.co.uk/hotlinks (express code 4233P) and click on the appropriate link.

- **Capital punishment:** find out more about capital punishment and its history in the UK.

- **Pro-capital punishment:** this site supports capital punishment and gives details of the prisoners currently on Death Row in the USA.

- **Justice:** find out more about this organisation, which campaigns for justice.

- **Alcoholism:** find out more about the effects of alcoholism from this website.

Student tips

I thought this topic was problematic because I felt I was being told what I should and shouldn't do with regard to drugs and alcohol and that wasn't what should be happening in class. However, my teacher made clear that this wasn't about forcing us to think and behave in particular ways, but describing the law and certain facts about alcohol and drug use and understanding how religions felt about them. It was up to us to make up our own mind about it for ourselves. I realised later that I learned some useful things and my attitudes to drugs and alcohol probably did change for the better.

Self-evaluation checklist

Read through the following list and evaluate how well you know and understand each of the topics.
How well have you understood the topics in this section? In the first column of the table below use the following code to rate your understanding:

Green – I understand this fully

Orange – I am confident I can answer most questions on this

Red – I need to do a lot more work on this topic.

In the second and third columns you need to think about:

● Whether you have an opinion on this topic and could give reasons for that opinion if asked

● Whether you can give the opinion of someone who disagrees with you and give reasons for this alternative opinion.

Content covered	My understanding is red/orange/green	Can I give my opinion?	Can I give an alternative opinion?
● The need for law and justice.			
● Theories of punishment and the arguments for and against them.			
● Why justice is important for Christians.			
● Why justice is important for Muslims.			
● The nature of capital punishment and non-religious arguments about capital punishment.			
● Different attitudes to capital punishment among Christians and the reasons for them.			
● Different attitudes to capital punishment for Muslims.			
● Laws on drugs and alcohol and the reasons for them.			
● Social and health problems caused by drugs and alcohol.			
● Different attitudes to drugs and alcohol in Christianity and the reasons for them.			
● Attitudes to drugs and alcohol in Islam.			

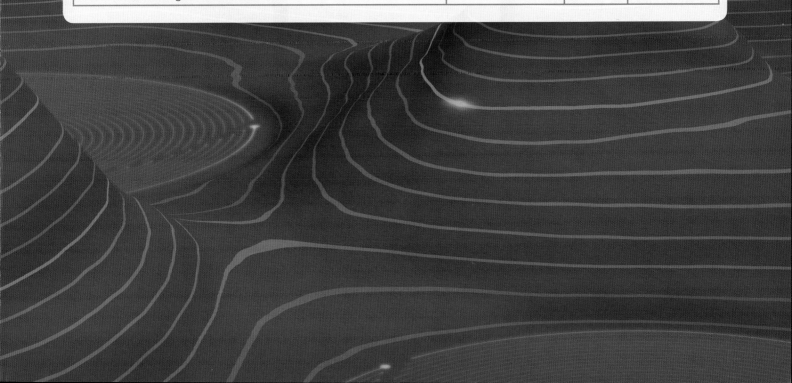

Introduction

In the exam you will see a choice of two questions on this section. Each question will include four tasks, which test your knowledge, understanding and evaluation of the material covered. A 2-mark question will ask you to define a term; a 4-mark question will ask your opinion on a point of view; an 8-mark question will ask you to explain a particular belief or idea; a 6-mark question will ask for your opinion on a point of view and ask you to consider an alternative point of view.

The word 'explain' means you should give clear reasons why Christians have different views on capital punishment, and show that you understand the reasoning behind those views. This question is worth 8 marks so you must be prepared to spend some time answering it. You will also be assessed on your use of language in this question.

Mini exam paper

(a) What is **crime**?
(2 marks)

(b) Do you think punishment is always right?

Give **two** reasons for your point of view. (4 marks)

(c) Explain why some Christians agree with capital punishment and some do not. (8 marks)

(d) 'It does not matter if religious people drink alcohol.'

In your answer you should refer to at least one religion.

(i) Do you agree? Give reasons for your opinion. (3 marks)

(ii) Give reasons why some people may disagree with you. (3 marks)

Here you need to give a short, accurate definition. You do not need to write more than one clear sentence

You can give your opinion, but make sure you do give two clear and thought out reasons. These can be ones you have learned in class, even if they are not your own opinion. You mustn't use terms such as 'rubbish' or 'stupid' as these don't show that you are able to think things through carefully.

Now you have to give the opposite point of view, again, using material you have learned during your studies. You must show you understand why people have these other views, even if you don't agree with them.

Don't make things up – use reasons you have learned in class. Don't forget to refer to a religion.

Mark scheme

(a) You will earn 2 marks for a correct answer, and 1 mark for a partially correct answer

(b) To earn up to the full 4 marks you need to give two reasons (as asked) and to develop them. Two brief reasons will earn 2 marks. One simple reason will only get 1 mark.

(c) You can earn 7–8 marks by giving up to four reasons, but the fewer reasons you give, the more you must develop them. You are being assessed on use of language, so you also need to take care to express your understanding in a clear style of English, and make some use of specialist vocabulary.

(d) To go beyond 3 marks for the whole of this question, you must refer to one religion. The more you are able to develop your answers the fewer reasons you will need to give. Three simple reasons can earn you the same mark as one fully developed reason.

ResultsPlus
Maximise your marks

(c) Explain why some Christians agree with capital punishment and some do not. (8 marks)

Student answer	Examiner comments	Improved student answer
Christians have different views on capital punishment based on what they think punishment should achieve. The message of Jesus is about forgiveness and giving people the chance to be reformed, but capital punishment makes this impossible since a dead person hasn't been given that chance. Also Christians believe life is sacred.	The answer starts well and the candidate offers a well developed reason why some Christians are against capital punishment. They then go on to give a second reason though this is not developed.	Christians have different views on capital punishment based on what they think punishment should achieve. The message of Jesus is about forgiveness and giving people the chance to be reformed, but capital punishment makes this impossible since a dead person hasn't been given that chance. Also Christians believe life is sacred and that only God has the right to take it away.
Other Christians, however, believe that capital punishment should be allowed by the state because it was used for many crimes in the Old Testament.	The candidate then goes on to look at the opposing view which is good, however they give just one reason which is not developed.	Other Christians, however, believe that capital punishment should be allowed by the state because it was used for many crimes in the Old Testament. Jesus never taught against capital punishment and some Churches support it for very serious crimes.

Welcome to examzone

Revising for your exams can be a daunting prospect. In this part of the book we'll take you through the best way of revising for your exams, step by step, to ensure you get the best results possible.

Zone In!

Have you ever become so absorbed in a task that suddenly it feels entirely natural and easy to perform? This is a feeling familiar to many athletes and performers. They work hard to recreate it in competition in order to do their very best. It's a feeling of being 'in the zone', and if you can achieve that same feeling in an examination, the chances are you'll perform brilliantly.

The good news is that you can get 'in the zone' by taking some simple steps in advance of the exam. Here are our top tips.

UNDERSTAND IT
Make sure you understand the exam process and what revision you need to do. This will give you confidence and also help you to get things into proportion. These pages are a good place to find some starting pointers for performing well in exams.

FRIENDS AND FAMILY

Make sure that your friends and family know when you want to revise. Even share your revision plan with them. Learn to control your times with them, so you don't get distracted. This means you can have better quality time with them when you aren't revising, because you aren't worrying about what you ought to be doing.

DEAL WITH DISTRACTIONS

Think about the issues in your life that may interfere with revision. Write them all down. Then think about how you can deal with each so they don't affect your revision.

COMPARTMENTALISE

You might not be able to deal with all the issues that can distract you. For example, you may be worried about a friend who is ill, or just be afraid of the exam. In this case, there is still a useful technique you can use. Put all of these worries into an imagined box in your mind at the start of your revision (or in the exam) and mentally lock it. Only open it again at the end of your revision session (or exam).

DIET AND EXERCISE

Make sure you eat sensibly and exercise as well! If your body is not in the right state, how can your mind be? A substantial breakfast will set you up for the day, and a light evening meal will keep your energy levels high.

BUILD CONFIDENCE
Use your revision time not only to revise content, but also to build your confidence in readiness for tackling the examination. For example, try tackling a short sequence of easy tasks in record time.

Planning Zone

The key to success in exams and revision often lies in good planning. Knowing **what** you need to do and **when** you need to do it is your best path to a stress-free experience. Here are some top tips in creating a great personal revision plan.

First of all, *know your strengths and weaknesses.*

Go through each topic making a list of how well you think you know the topic. Use your mock examination results and/or any other test results that are available as a check on your self-assessment. This will help you to plan your personal revision effectively, putting extra time into your weaker areas.

Next, *create your plan!*

Remember to make time for considering how topics interrelate.

For example, in PE you will be expected to know not just about the various muscles, but how these relate to various body types.

The specification quite clearly states when you are expected to be able to link one topic to another so plan this into your revision sessions.

You will be tested on this in the exam and you can gain valuable marks by showing your ability to do this.

Finally, *follow the plan!*

You can use the revision sections in the following pages to kick-start your revision.

MAY

SUNDAY	MONDAY	TUESD
30	30	1

Be realistic about how much time you can devote to your revision, but also make sure you put in enough time. Give yourself regular breaks or different activities to give your life some variance. Revision need not be a prison sentence!

Find out your exam dates. Go to the Edexcel website **www.edexcel.com** to find all final exam dates, and check with your teacher.

view Sectio
complete tw
ractice exa
questions

13

Chunk your revision in each subject down into smaller sections. This will make it more manageable and less daunting.

Draw up a list of all the dates from the start of your revision right through to your exams.

Review Sectio
complete three
practice exam
. . . . ns

20

Review Sectio
Try the Keywor
Quiz again

Make sure you allow time for assessing your progress against your initial self-assessment. Measuring progress will allow you to see and be encouraged by your improvement. These little victories will build your confidence.

22

EXAM DAY!

27

28

29

Know Zone
Topic 1: Rights and responsibilities

In this section, you need to show the examiner not only that you have a good understanding of the different authorities Christians use to make moral decisions, but also that you understand why different Christians use different authorities. You need to show you understand why it is that Christians can have differing beliefs about moral authorities and yet all still be genuinely Christian. The rest of this section deals with human rights and genetic engineering, and how Christians respond to the moral questions these topics raise. Again, you need to be able to evaluate why different Christians respond in different ways.

As part of the AO2 assessment you also have to be able to explain your own views and assess why and how they differ from other views. The issue here is that you can be critical of your own views and those of others and recognise the variety of beliefs that can be held about the same issues.

Revision

Look back at the KnowZone at the end of the section on page 26. Read through the Checklist and identify your stronger and weaker areas, so that you can focus on those areas you are less confident about. You might like to try the Quick quiz or the Plenary activity at the end of the section, or the Support activity below. When you are ready for some exam practice, read through the exam zone on pages 28–29. Then you could attempt the questions opposite.

Support activity

Make yourself a revision table. Write down the different moral authorities used by Christians – the Bible, the Church, conscience and Situation Ethics in the first column. Then in the second column briefly explain what each one means. Divide the third column into different types of Christians, such as Catholic Christians, Traditional Christians and Liberal Christians, and then write what each of these would say about each moral authority. Finally, in the last column write down your own opinions on each moral authority. For each one, assess whether you think it provides a good way of making moral decisions. Once you have finished making this table, you can use it as a reminder just before the exam.

Practice exam questions

a) What is the 'Golden Rule'? (2 marks)

b) Do you think human rights need more protection in the United Kingdom?

   Give two reasons for your point of view. (4 marks)

c) Explain how Christians make moral decisions. (8 marks)

d) 'Christians should agree with cloning.' In your answer you should refer to Christianity.

   (i)   Do you agree? Give reasons for your opinion. (3 marks)

   (ii) Give reasons why some people may disagree with you. (3 marks)

The material in this section concerns serious problems that affect everyone in the world today. Firstly, you need to ensure that you understand what each of the issues are: global warming, pollution, natural resources, infertility treatments and transplant surgery. Then you need to demonstrate to the examiner that you can view these issues through the eyes of religious believers, even if these views are different from your own. To gain the highest marks you need to understand what makes these views distinctive for religious believers – for example, the belief that God created the world and wants people to take care of it. As with other sections you also need to be able to express your own views on these issues and demonstrate that you understand alternative views.

Revision

Look back at the KnowZone at the end of the section on page 54. Read through the Checklist and think about which your stronger and weaker areas are, so that you can focus on those areas you are less confident about. You might like to try the Quick quiz or the Plenary activity at the end of the section, or the Support activity below. When you are ready for some exam practice, read through the exam zone on pages 56–57. Then you could attempt the questions opposite.

Support activity

Do some Internet research to find out more about what religious believers are doing to help the environment. These will be useful as examples to use in the exam, which will gain you extra marks.

Practice exam questions

a) What is stewardship? (2 marks)

b) Do you think global warming is a big problem?

   Give two reasons for your point of view. (4 marks)

c) Explain why some Christians agree with fertility treatments and some do not. (8 marks)

d) 'All religious people should carry a donor card.'

   In your answer you should refer to at least one religion.

   (i) Do you agree? Give reasons for your opinion. (3 marks)

   (ii) Give reasons why some people may disagree with you. (3 marks)

Know Zone
Topic 3: Peace and conflict

Remember that this section is about conflict at all levels from international wars to conflicts within families. In many cases, you can apply the religious teachings to these issues, so be sure that you know what they are and how different people within each religion view conflict and try to resolve it. As with all the sections, be sure that you know the key words and their definitions inside out as this will really help you in the exam! Also remember that you need to give your own opinions on this issues and they must be backed up with reasons – you will receive low marks if, although you can say *what* you think, you cannot say *why* you think it. It is equally important to be able to explain those views that are different to yours and why some people, particularly religious believers, have these views.

Revision

Look back at the KnowZone at the end of the section on page 82. Read through the Checklist and think about which your stronger and weaker areas are, so that you can focus on those areas you are less confident about. You might like to try the Quick quiz or the Plenary activity at the end of the section, or the Support activity below. When you are ready for some exam practice, read through the exam zone on pages 84–85. Then you could attempt the questions opposite.

Support activity

Look back at pages 60 and 62, which are about the Darfur conflict. Either choose this conflict or, if you prefer, choose another conflict that is either happening at the moment or is very recent, and do some research to find out more about it. What were the different factors that caused the war? How did the United Nations respond? How have different religious believers responded to this conflict?

Practice exam questions

a) What is pacifism? (2 marks)

b) Do you think schools treat bullies too softly?

Give two reasons for your point of view. (4 marks)

c) Choose one religion other than Christianity and explain why forgiveness is important for the followers of that religion. (8 marks)

d) 'If people were more religious, there would be no wars.'

In your answer you should refer to at least one religion.

(i) Do you agree? Give reasons for your opinion. (3 marks)

(ii) Give reasons why some people may disagree with you. (3 marks)

Rather like all of the topics in this book, the issues you study in this section are ones of public concern, not just of concern to religious believers. Your task in the exam is to show that you understand how different people, including religious believers, tackle issues of law and justice, capital punishment, and drugs and alcohol. It is important to remember that, within each religion, there are different opinions on these issues. You need to be able to explain both *what* these are and *why* people have these views. As always you should be able to demonstrate that you can see all points of view, whatever your own opinions are.

Revision

Look back at the KnowZone at the end of the section on page 110. Read through the Checklist and think about which your stronger and weaker areas are, so that you can focus on those areas you are less confident about. You might like to try the Quick quiz or the Plenary activity at the end of the section, or the Support activity below. When you are ready for some exam practice, read through the exam zone on pages 112–113. Then you could attempt the questions opposite.

Support activity

To help you to explain the different opinions people have on these issues, divide into small groups and carry out a survey. For example, ask your family and friends what they think about capital punishment? Do they think it's a good idea or not? In what circumstances, if any, would they agree with it? Remember to ask them to give reasons for their beliefs. Then present your findings to the class.

Practice exam questions

a) What is a sin? (2 marks)

b) Do you agree with capital punishment? Give two reasons for your point of view. (4 marks)

c) Choose one religion other than Christianity, and explain why justice is important for the followers of that religion. (8 marks)

d) 'Religious people should always obey the law.'

   In your answer you should refer to at least one religion.

   (i) Do you agree? Give reasons for your opinion. (3 marks)

   (ii) Give reasons why some people may disagree with you. (3 marks)

Don't Panic Zone

As you get close to completing your revision, the Big Day will be getting nearer and nearer. Many students find this the most stressful time and tend to go into panic mode, either working long hours without really giving their brains a chance to absorb information, or giving up and staring blankly at the wall.

Panicking simply makes your brain seize up and you find that information and thoughts simply cannot flow naturally. You become distracted and anxious, and things seem worse than they are. Many students build the exams up into more than they are. Remember: the exams are not trying to catch you out! If you have studied the course, there will be no surprises on the exam paper!

Student tip

I know how silly it is to panic, especially if you've done the work and know your stuff. I was asked by a teacher to produce a report on a project I'd done, and I panicked so much I spent the whole afternoon crying and worrying. I asked other people for help, but they were panicking too. In the end, I calmed down and looked at the task again. It turned out to be quite straightforward and, in the end, I got my report finished first and it was the best of them all!

In the exam you don't have much time, so you can't waste it by panicking. The best way to control panic is simply to do what you have to do. Think carefully for a few minutes, then start writing and as you do, the panic will drain away.

Don't panic

Exam Zone

You will have an one-and-a-half hours for this exam paper and in that time you have to answer **four** questions, one on each of the four sections you have studied: Rights and responsibilities, Environmental and medical issues, Peace and conflict, and Crime and punishment.

In each section, you can make a choice from two questions.

Each question will be made up of four different parts.

- A 2-mark question will ask you to define a term
- a 4-mark question will ask your opinion on a point of view
- an 8-mark question will ask you to explain a particular belief or idea
- a 6-mark question will ask for your opinion on a point of view and ask you to consider an alternative point of view.

Effectively you shouldn't spend more than 22.5 minutes on each section (that's 90 minutes divided by 4):

- the 8-mark question deserves the most attention, so that's around 9 minutes
- the 2-mark question should take you 1.5 minutes, then
- 5 minutes for the 4-mark question, and
- the remaining 7 minutes for the 6-mark question.

Obviously you can give or take here or there, and your teacher may guide you differently, but as long as you don't go over 22.5 minutes altogether and the length of each of your answers is appropriate for the number of marks available, then you'll be on the right lines.

Meet the exam paper

This diagram shows the front cover of the exam paper. These instructions, information and advice will always appear on the front of the paper. It is worth reading it carefully now. Check you understand it. Now is a good opportunity to ask your teacher about anything you are not sure of here.

Print your surname here, and your other names afterwards. This is an additional safeguard to ensure that the exam board awards the marks to the right candidate.

Here you fill in the school's exam number.

Ensure that you understand exactly how long the examination will last, and plan your time accordingly.

Note that the quality of your written communication will also be marked. Take particular care to present your thoughts and work at the highest standard you can, for maximum marks.

Here you fill in your personal exam number. Take care when writing it down because the number is important to the exam board when writing your score.

In this box, the examiner will write the total marks you have achieved in the exam paper.

Make sure that you understand exactly which questions from which sections you should attempt.

Don't feel that you have to fill the answer space provided. Everybody's handwriting varies, so a long answer from you may take up as much space a short answer from someone else.

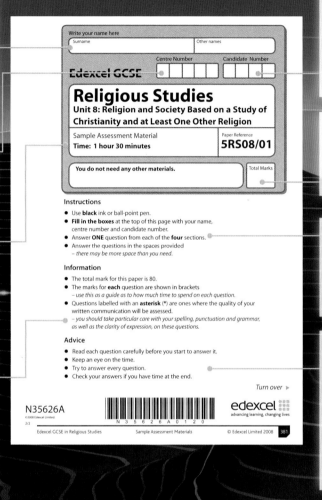

Write your name here

Surname

Other names

Centre Number

Candidate Number

Edexcel GCSE

Religious Studies

Unit 8: Religion and Society Based on a Study of Christianity and at Least One Other Religion

Sample Assessment Material
Time: 1 hour 30 minutes

Paper Reference
5RS08/01

You do not need any other materials.

Total Marks

Instructions

- Use **black** ink or ball-point pen.
- **Fill in the boxes** at the top of this page with your name, centre number and candidate number.
- Answer **ONE** question from each of the **four** sections.
- Answer the questions in the spaces provided
  – there may be more space than you need.

Information

- The total mark for this paper is 80.
- The marks for **each** question are shown in brackets
  – use this as a guide as to how much time to spend on each question.
- Questions labelled with an **asterisk** (*) are ones where the quality of your written communication will be assessed.
  – you should take particular care with your spelling, punctuation and grammar, as well as the clarity of expression, on these questions.

Advice

- Read each question carefully before you start to answer it.
- Keep an eye on the time.
- Try to answer every question.
- Check your answers if you have time at the end.

Turn over ▶

N35626A
©2008 Edexcel Limited.
2/2

Edexcel GCSE in Religious Studies   Sample Assessment Materials   © Edexcel Limited 2008   381

edexcel
advancing learning, changing lives

Practical tips on the exam paper

- You must use a black pen. Your paper is scanned into a computer for marking. If you write in any other colour, you risk your work not being seen clearly.

- You must choose your question carefully – cross out the one you are not going to do – to avoid changing a question half-way through answering it. This is a very common mistake and costs candidates lots of marks!

- Mark with an x at the top of the page which question you have chosen.

- Do not write outside the guidelines – your answer may get cut off by the scanning process.

- Do not use extra sheets and attach them unless it is absolutely necessary. If you need more space – for example, for a (b) question – continue into the (c) space and when you change question write your own (c). Do the same for (c) into (d). If you then run out, put an arrow and write at the end of the exam booklet.

Zone Out

About your grades

Whether you've done better than, worse than, or just as you expected, your grades are the final measure of your performance on your course and in the exams. On this page we explain some of the information that appears on your results slip and tell you what to do if you think something is wrong. We answer the most popular questions about grades and look at some of the options facing you.

When will my results be published?

Results for summer examinations are issued on the **middle** two Thursdays in August, with GCE first and GCSE second. November exam results are issued in January, January exam results are issued in March and March exam results issued in April.

Can I get my results online?

Visit **www.resultsplusdirect.co.uk**, where you will find detailed student results information including the 'Edexcel Gradeometer' which demonstrates how close you were to the nearest grade boundary.

I haven't done as well as I expected. What can I do now?

First of all, talk to your subject teacher. After all the teaching that you have had, tests and internal examinations, he/she is the person who best knows what grade you are capable of achieving. Take your results slip to your subject teacher, and go through the information on it in detail. If you both think there is something wrong with the result, the school or college can apply to see your completed examination paper and then, if necessary, ask for a re-mark immediately. The original mark can be confirmed or lowered, as well as raised, as a result of a re-mark.

How do my grades compare with those of everybody else who sat this exam?

You can compare your results with those of others in the UK who have completed the same examination using the information on Edexcel website at **www.Edexcel.com**

I achieved a higher mark for the same unit last time. Can I use that result?

Yes. The higher score is the one that goes towards your overall grade. Even if you sat a unit more than twice, the best result will be used automatically when the overall grade is calculated. You do not need to ask the exam board to take into account a previous result. This will be done automatically so you can be assured that all your best unit results have gone into calculating your overall grade.

What happens if I was ill over the period of my examinations?

If you become ill before or during the examination period you are eligible for special consideration. This also applies if you have been affected by an accident, bereavement or serious disturbance during an examination.

If my school has requested special consideration for me, is this shown on my Statement of Results?

If your school has requested special consideration for you, it is not shown on your results slip, but it will be shown on a subject mark report that is sent to your school or college. If you want to know whether special consideration was requested for you, you should ask your Examinations Officer.

Can I have a re-mark of my examination paper?

Yes, this is possible, but remember that only your school or college can apply for a re-mark, not you or your parents/carers. First of all, you should consider carefully whether or not to ask your school or college to make a request for a re-mark. It is worth knowing that very few re-marks result in a change to a grade – not because Edexcel is embarrassed that a change of marks has been made, but simply because a re-mark request has shown that the original marking was accurate. Check the closing date for re-marking requests with your Examinations Officer.

When I asked for a re-mark of my paper, my subject grade went down. What can I do?

There is no guarantee that your grades will go up if your papers are re-marked. They can also go down or stay the same. After a re-mark, the only way to improve your grade is to take the examination again. Your school or college Examinations Officer can tell you when you can do that.

How many times can I re-sit a unit?

You may resit a modular GCSE Science or Mathematics module test once, prior to taking your terminal examination and before obtaining your final overall grade. The highest score obtained on either the first attempt or the re-sit counts towards your final grade. If you enter a module in GCSE Mathematics at a different tier, this does not count as a re-sit. If you are on the full modular Religious Studies GCSE course, and sat the first unit last year, you may re-sit module 1 when you sit module 2 to maximise your full course grade.

For much more information, visit www.examzone.co.uk

Glossary

This is an extended glossary containing definitions that will help you in your studies. Edexcel key terms are not included as all of these are defined in the lessons themselves.

abortion – The removal of a foetus from the womb before it can survive.

acid rain – Rain, hail or snow that contains pollutants, such as sulphur and nitrogen compounds.

adultery – A sexual act between a married person and someone other than their marriage partner.

atheism – Believing that God does not exist.

authority – Power over others through position or moral teaching.

Catechism – An elementary manual of Christian doctrine.

conflict – Stresses and strains that take place within all human relationships.

conscientious objector – A person who objects to military service because their conscience tells them that it is wrong to fight or kill other people.

conversion – Where a person changes from one religion to another, or a non-believer becomes a believer.

crucifixion – The Roman death penalty suffered by Jesus when he was nailed to the cross.

designer baby – A baby that has been genetically engineered to have no defects, or to have features that the parents want.

DNA – An acid present in all plant and animal cells that is the means of passing on hereditary characteristics.

dominion – Power and authority over others.

ethics – A system of morals and rules of behaviour.

Eucharist *see* **Holy Communion**

fatwa – A legal opinion or guidance of a knowledgeable Muslim scholar, based on the Qur'an, Shari'ah law and other sources.

foetus – An unborn baby at least eight weeks old.

fossil fuels – Fuels such as oil, coal, etc. that were produced in the earth over millions of years as animal and plant matter decayed and was preserved in rocks.

Fundamentalists – Christians who believe in the literal truth of the Bible.

hadith – The sayings and actions of the Prophet Muhammad as recorded by his family and friends.

hajj – The annual pilgrimage to Mecca (Makkah), which each Muslim must undertake at least once in a lifetime if he or she has the health or wealth.

Holocaust – Destruction or murder on a mass scale, especially that of Jews under the German Nazi regime in the Second World War.

Holy Communion – A Christian service in which bread and wine are consumed, recalling the Last Supper and celebrating the death and resurrection of Jesus Christ.

interest (money) – Extra money that has to be paid to the lender when money is borrowed.

khalifah – A custodian or steward of the world for Allah.

Last Supper – The supper taken by Jesus and his disciples on the eve of his crucifixion.

litter – Rubbish, especially food containers or wrappers, that is carelessly dropped in a public place.

lobbying – Campaigning to try and influence public officials or Members of Parliament.

Mecca (Makkah) – The birthplace of the Prophet Muhammad, to which a pilgrimage, the hajj, is made every year.

New Testament – The second part of the Bible, which records the life of Jesus and the early Church.

nuclear weapons – Weapons based on atomic fission or fusion.

Old Testament – The first part of the Bible, which Christians believe foretells the coming of Jesus.

parable – A story of something that might have happened, told to illustrate a moral issue or duty.

Parliament – The body of political representatives of a country, in the UK consisting of the House of Commons, where MPs sit, and the House of Lords.

pilgrimage – A journey to a holy place or shrine.

Plymouth Brethren – A strict religious body, founded in Dublin in about 1825, whose first meeting was held in Plymouth, Devon in 1831.

Pope – The Bishop of Rome, head of the Roman Catholic Church.

Protestant – That part of the Christian Church that became distinct from the Roman Catholic and other churches, when their members 'protested' the centrality of the Bible and other beliefs.

Quaker – A member of the Religious Society of Friends, established through the work of George Fox in the 17th century.

Qur'an – The sacred book of Islam.

Roman Catholic – That part of the Christian Church owing loyalty to the Pope in Rome.

sanction – A military or economic measure taken by one country in order to persuade another country to follow a certain course of action.

sanctity of life – The belief that life is holy and belongs to God.

secular – Non-religious.

Sermon on the Mount – Jesus' description of Christian living.

Shari'ah law – Law based on the Qur'an, the teachings of Muhammad and the work of Islamic scholars.

Surah – A division of the Qur'an.

terrorism – An organised system of terror, usually violent, used to achieve political ends.

ummah – The worldwide Muslim community.

vandalism – Senseless damage to other people's property or to the environment.

Zakah – The tax that Muslims pay for the poor.

Index

In the following index, main entries of key terms are given in **bold** type and the page number that is also in bold will lead you to a definition of the word. For further definitions of unfamiliar words, see also the Glossary on pages 124–25.